Dreams
and
Reality

New Era of China's Reform

Dreams

and

Reality

New Era of China's Reform

Editor

Jian Ping

DePaul University, USA

World Scientific

中央编译出版社
Central Compilation & Translation Press

Published by

World Scientific Publishing Co. Pte. Ltd.

5 Toh Tuck Link, Singapore 596224

USA office: 27 Warren Street, Suite 401-402, Hackensack, NJ 07601

UK office: 57 Shelton Street, Covent Garden, London WC2H 9HE

and

Central Compilation and Translation Press
Room 302B, Part B Hongru Building
#B-5 Chegongzhuang Street Xicheng
District, Beijing 100044, China

Library of Congress Cataloging-in-Publication Data
Names: Jian, Ping, 1960– editor.
Title: Dreams and reality : new era of China's reform / Jian Ping.
Description: New Jersey : World Scientific, [2016]
Identifiers: LCCN 2015036788 | ISBN 9789814651967
Subjects: LCSH: China--Economic policy--2000– | China--Politics and government--2002– |
  China--Foreign economic relations. | China--Foreign relations--21st century.
Classification: LCC HC427.95 .D74 2016 | DDC 338.951--dc23
LC record available at http://lccn.loc.gov/2015036788

British Library Cataloguing-in-Publication Data
A catalogue record for this book is available from the British Library.

This edition is jointly published by World Scientific Publishing Co. Pte. Ltd. and Central Compilation and Translation Press. This edition is distributed worldwide by World Scientific Publishing Co. Pte. Ltd., except China.

Typeset in China

Printed in China

Preface

The 60 years since the founding of the People's Republic of China, especially the 30 years of reform and opening up, have witnessed glorious achievements in China, as well as some difficulties and challenges. How China will develop and how the Chinese Dream will come true have become a global focus and a hot topic in recent years.

Central Compilation & Translation Press has invited a number of renowned scholars at home and abroad to provide analyses of the status quo and projections of the future development trends of China. Covering the areas of the society, economy, politics, culture and the environment, their analyses and projections have pointed out the concerns that should draw all our attention. The significance of publishing this book lies in proposing an issue that China and other countries must focus on: What does China's future development mean to the world order? On the part of China, it is because it's directly concerned with China's global strategy and orientation; on the part of the other countries, it is because China plays a very important role in the global development.

The world is undergoing a great change. What China will look like in 2049 will be determined by how we are going to understand today's world, evaluate the trends of recent years, and respond to the existing and upcoming challenges. We wish to hear the opinions of people from different areas across the world, and make this book a basis for extensive debates. We wish it to be helpful to those who expect to understand and build a common goal. We also hope that the publication of this book may provoke more challenges and secure more suggestions, in order to tackle the challenges that will be part of China's future and the world's future. The trends and challenges China is going to face in the future will be complicated and formidable, which will influence the whole world and will not be solved without the intelligence of experts from all over the world.

Most of the articles contained in the book were exclusively solicited by the Press, and some, which were already published in Chinese, were revised when included in this book. We would like to take this opportunity to thank all the authors for their great support.

About the editor

Jian Ping is a contributing writer at *Xinhua News* and *China Daily*, and is a columnist for *Asian Wisconzine*, a monthly magazine in the Midwest of America. She is an adjunct professor at DePaul University in Chicago and a member of the China Committee, Chicago Sister Cities International. She also works as a U.S.-China business consultant and is responsible for setting up the collaboration between Chicago WFMT Radio Network and various entities in China, in which major classical music programs from the U.S. are introduced to China via radio stations, and music festivals in China are produced and introduced to the West — groundbreaking for Chinese music programs to be systematically broadcast on radio stations across North America and many countries in Europe. She is the author of *Mulberry Child: A Memoir of China*, which has been developed into a feature-length award winning documentary movie of the same title (*Mulberry Child*) in the U.S.

Contents

1

China in 2030

Kerry Brown

Kerry Brown
Professor of Chinese Politics and Director of the China Studies Centre at the University of Sydney. He leads the Europe China Research and Advice Network (ECRAN) funded by the European Union and is an Associate Fellow on the Asia Programme at Chatham House, London. His main interests are in the politics and society of modern China, in its international relations and its political economy.

In the coming two decades, China will be facing demographic, economic, environmental and political challenges. In any one of these four areas, mishandling by the government would create instability which will impact dramatically not just China, but the rest of the world.

China's inherent instability should not be underestimated. While its economic success since 1978 has been justly celebrated, the task from now onwards of moving away from creating simply GDP growth to addressing some of the problems that this rapid growth has created will grow far harder.

The position of the Communist Party of China (CPC, also CCP) is critical. It remains fundamentally in charge of the key areas of policy decision making in the PRC. But in the coming decade, it will need to come up with a positive strategy to deliver greater legal reform, and of dealing with civil society in ways that can fully embrace the benefits of these groups within society. The Party's ability to cope with these major issues will define the nature of its rule up to and beyond 2030, and the stability and viability of China as a state thereafter.

After over 60 years in power, the Communist Party of China goes deeper into the 21st century as the master of almost all it surveys. Having made a pact with business people in 2001 by allowing them back into the Party, it has seen off every major threat to its power. With 80 million members, it is the largest political party in the history of humanity, and one of the most formidable political forces of the 21st century. It maintains control over the People's Liberation Army (PLA) and over the other areas of significant power in society.

And yet the Party finds itself facing a series of challenges, any one of which, if it mishandles them, will fundamentally threaten its hold on power. In the coming decades, it will need fresh ideas and approaches on how to face the massive challenges facing the country it rules in terms of sustainability and stability. Public opinion within China on the environment, economic issues, and China's role in the world, are varied, and constantly impact on government policy. Social media, like *Weibo*, have illustrated this, with over 300 million users now, showing the complexity of opinions within contemporary Chinese society and the real difficulty to creating consensus.

The Party is no longer allowed the luxury during the Maoist era of having unquestioned, untrammelled power. It has to choose its territory carefully these days. Chinese elite leaders like Premier Wen Jiabao have talked of their anxiety over the rise in social unrest and mass protests since 2001. Even so, the institutions and structures in society to deal with a rise in conflict between different provincial and national level groups and their competing demands on elite interest, resources and power have never been under greater pressure. According to Yu Jianrong, a professor at the Chinese Academic of Social Sciences, in 2009 there were over 100,000 incidents of mass unrest. In 2009, according to another statistic, there were 9 million petitions to the central government, over issues ranging from land rights to pension rights for discharged military officers and those laid off in the past from state-owned enterprises. We can say, therefore, that in the era in which China has grown increasingly rich as a country, it has also seen the same kinds of social contention and conflict that others have experienced.

The leaders of the CPC have said that they wish to achieve a special form of democracy for China by 2050. They have not stated clearly what this form of democracy might be. They have, however, made clear that models available from either Europe or other Asian countries do not appeal to China's specific social and developmental complexity. In his speech at the 2007 17th Party Congress Hu Jintao used the word 'democracy' over 60 times. Chinese leaders now speak about democracy with a level of confidence never seen before. They even issued a White Paper on Democracy in 2005. But the meaning of democracy in these documents and speeches is highly circumscribed. It is clear that the CPC is not attracted by multi-party western models of governance. Instead, the CPC wishes to create genuine competition within itself, and to cut away the risk of instability that it associates with representative forms of democracy that are available elsewhere. It appeals to Chinese people's strong memories of instability and weakness from when the CPC came to power in 1949. The CPC has linked itself with stability, and has presented itself as the country's one true guardian of this.

But there are key areas where public demands on the quality of the CPC governance are becoming more exacting. The Party's ability to allow participation in decision making, to create a meaningful rule of law, to deliver social justice, and to improve good governance will all have a key impact on its ability to remain in power. These are things that President and Party Secretary Hu Jintao recognised in his speech to the 17th Party Congress in 2007. In two areas, within the next 20 years, it must make fundamental changes to its current mode of behaviour, and move from a simple 'co-option' strategy which it practices at the moment, to something which is more positive and meets the natural expectations of a more sophisticated and demanding public. These are the creation of a genuine rule of law, and tolerance of genuine civil society groups. Party control and involvement in both of these areas at the moment is obvious. But the ability of the Party to continue to pretend that there will not come a moment when courts in China will start to challenge the government's decision making, and fundamentally oppose it, are limited. Like other transitional societies, it is approaching the moment when courts will start to hold the Party to laws passed by its own government. When this happens, the Party has the decision to either oppose this, or to accept it and move forward in a wholly new environment where its fundamental legitimacy to rule is redefined. In the last five years, there have been elements in the Party that have attacked the ability of lawyers to challenge the CPC's legitimacy. They have said that they will not allow this to happen. The role of civil society as a 'virus' by which to carry into the Chinese body politic other ways of challenging the Party's predominance has also created problems. Huge numbers of NGOs and civil society groups have been established in the last two decades. In some cities, civil society groups have been contracted to deliver government services. And yet the Party remains suspicious of some of these groups, and lets them exist in a legal limbo where their status is unclear, and, as has been proved by the arrest and imprisonment of civil society leaders who protested over the Sichuan earthquake problems last year, it is ready, and willing, to use legal instruments to silence those who are seen as challenging it in key areas.

In the next 20 years, sooner than either it predicts, or many outsiders allow, the CPC will need to deliver fundamental political reforms. It will need to have a positive strategy to deal with the existence of genuinely independent courts able to challenge its judgments, and it will need to spell out more clearly the legitimate role of civil society. It will also need to have a strategy to deal with the existence of real political opposition. The current strategy to do this by incorporating everyone into the Party is unsustainable. There will come a time when some form of organised political opposition will appear. The Party will need to have thought through the risks of continuing to crush this, and facing a potential backlash, which will create the very instability that it most fears. How the Party responds in this 'do or die' moment will dictate how China as a country fares in the coming two decades. If the Party toughs it out, then the chances of real instability and social upheaval are high. If it makes a pragmatic pact, and engages in this process, its chances of survival are good, even though it will rule on different terms to the first few decades of its existence.

China needs to undertake political reform because of the massive complexity of the issues it is facing in the coming two decades, and the fact that it is trying to now get ready for these with a highly centralised system that was largely borrowed in the middle of the 20th century from the Soviet Union. The Party's inability to create consensus even within its own elite on key issues like economic development, climate change, and legal reform, are worrying. Within society, a vast number of websites, blogs, and magazines testify to the rich variety of opinion within China. The government needs to have better means of demonstrating public support for key policy decisions, rather than just rhetoric. And there have to be ways of allowing public input into governance so that the high levels of public dissatisfaction with corruption, the environment, and inequality can be addressed.

There are some issues that can already be predicted with some certainty, even by 2020. China's demographics by this period are deeply problematic. Gender imbalance is already critical, with 106 men for 100 women, and, in some rural areas, 140 men to 100 women. China is looking at having 20 to 30 million single men by 2020. The impact of the one child policy means that China is also facing an abrupt aging population crisis, with two people of working age then supporting one person who is retired. Changing composition of the family structure means that the normal networks to support the aged and other dependents will have been eroded. In the next decade China will have to create a whole social security network in places and ways it currently doesn't have.

By 2025, China will have become the world's largest user of all energy resources, and may well use more than the rest of the world put together. But despite a major nuclear power station building programme (30 by 2020), and increased use of renewable resources, it will remain fundamentally reliant on fossil fuels, and in particular on coal. This is intimately linked to its environmental problems. China's hunger for energy will bring it into competition with other countries like Central Asia, Africa and Latin America. Its energy hunger will also mean that it will need to look at creating a wholly different kind of economic model, shifting away from manufacturing, export led growth to a higher value, less energy inefficient and more internally consumer driven model. In particular, dramatic increases in car usage and in urbanisation will create increasingly unsustainable strains on China's natural environment, calling for radical new forms of technology long before 2030. And by 2030, China will have answered its currently greatest challenge — water supply and clean water sources. 70% of China's water is now reckoned to be polluted, with large parts of the north east suffering prolonged droughts, and cities like Beijing and Shanghai suffering severe lack of supply of fresh water.

The current leadership of China comes from a very narrow and specific political culture. They are servants of the party, owe all they are to the party, and have been brought up and created by it. But in their handling of key strategic issues they have to show an ability to communicate with society in ways which, much like western politicians, sell policy options to them, and convince them of the need to support the government, even as it undertakes some difficult changes which may well work against the interests of some groups in society and for others. They are cautious, believe in gradualism, but they are also instinctively aware of the long history of instability that has afflicted China for many centuries. This only ties their hands even further.

The current political system in China will not be in place in 2030. By that time, there will be a different model, one in which the party is likely (but not certain) to be dominant, but in which major areas will have been ceded to civil society and to other political players. If the CPC is intelligent in how it makes these compromises, then China's ability to continue to exist as a strong, unified country is high. But mismanagement of its responses to any of the key areas above, and particularly to political reform, could result in the dreaded outcome of breakdown, social upheaval, and failure. Because of the profound integration of China into the global economy the impact of this not just for China but the rest of the world could be devastating. For this reason, China remains a major threat to world stability, not because of aggressive external intent, but because of its own vulnerabilities and fracture lines.

2

The Rise of China and

the Restructuring of World Order[1]

Zhu Yunhan

Zhu Yunhan

Born in Taipei in 1956, Prof. Zhu Yunhan graduated from the Department of Political Science, National Taiwan University in 1977, received his master's degree in Political Science from the National Taiwan University in 1979 and his Ph.D in Political Science from the University of Minnesota in 1987. As one of the Taiwan scholars of political science with high international reputation, he is presently the Distinguished Research Fellow of the Preparatory Office, Institute of Political Science at Academia Sinica, professor of the Department of Political Science, National Taiwan University, and Executive Director of Taiwan Chiang Ching-kuo Foundation for International Scholarly Exchange. He was elected as Academician of Academia Sinica in July 2012. His research focuses include the

---

[1] This article is based on the record of the lecture delivered by the author for a general-education course in the National Taiwan University in November 2012.

the democratization and methodology of social sciences.

"The rise of China is one of the most important transforming forces shocking the present world structure, and will be one of the forces leading the restructuring of the world order in the 21st century. In this sense, China's model of development will influence the restructuring of the world order, and China's path of development will influence the future of the human community."

—Zhu Yunhan

challenge of the 21st century is how to understand the rise of China in a historical context. The rise of China and the emergence of China's development model is a massive historical change to the whole world.

China's fast economic growth is unprecedented and very probably unparalleled in the future, in the history of mankind. This is the most widespread industrialization ever: there has never been any other country or society that has gone through industrialization on such a scale and at such speed. How has this unprecedented rise become possible? Simply speaking, the China model has three unique qualities: the first is the "institutional" advantage in China; the second is China has exerted its advantage of being "great"; and the third is the advantage of China being a "latecomer" in the era of globalization.

The rise of China must be interpreted in a macro-history scenario, from which we may interpret that the change over the last 60 years only represents China's recovering its quota in the world economic system and its position in East Asia, and from which we should interpret the rise of China as a part of the big story of "the all-round rise of the non-western world," the big story itself being the main plotline of the historical change of the world from the last four decades of the 20th century to the beginning of the 21st century. It is inevitable for the global productivity to redistribute and for wealth to bring about the change in the power landscape and ideological structure. The all-round rise of the non-western world also means that the human community will be facing two possible historical development situations at the same time. On the one hand, the world order may enter a long period of disintegration and restructuring, during which it is hard to avoid disorder and chaos to some degree and many public governance issues at the global level may be put aside almost for good. On the other hand, we may be welcoming the arrival of a more just world order: an international economic exchange model better reflecting the principle of equality and reciprocity, and a global sphere for public discussion showing more respect for cultural and religious pluralism; a world order that serves the need for sustainable development of the majority on the earth and a world order that together and enjoy harmony through diversity.

The Rise of China and Its Future Role

To picture China's future role in the world, we may start with a book titled *Eclipse*, with the subtitle of "Living in the Shadow of China's Economic Dominance."[1] Published in September 2011, the book stirred a very hot discussion in Washington. The author of the book is Arvind Subramanian, an Indian American, who is a senior research fellow of the Institute for International Economics, a famous think tank in America. This book provides serious analysis and projections of the economic structure of the future world. It has a very dramatic opening, an imagined scene, so as to attract readers' attention. The opening reads as follows: The American government faces a fiscal bankruptcy in 2021. The American president drives on Pennsylvania Avenue, the one passing in front of the White House and leading to Capital Hill, and arrives at the International Monetary Fund at the other end of the avenue, where he signs a bail-out agreement with a corporate president of Chinese nationality and obtains a loan of 3 trillion dollars for urgent financing, and meanwhile promises that America is going to follow a series of conditions. Those conditions may resemble those that Greece and Spain must accept under coercion when they sought bail-outs. He puts a full stop to this scene, which is, of course, fictitious. He says, "At this moment, the ceremony of handing over the power of leading the world has been completed." This is the prologue of the book.

This scene, though fictitious, is not absolutely impossible. Subramanian's analysis, based on a very complete structure, is concerned with the global economic structure. Based on the change of world economic structure since 1870, including the different GDP percentages, trade volume and capital flow among different countries, he believes that China is now in a critical period of replacing the dominant position of America in the world economy.

---

[1] Arvind Subramanian, *Eclipse: Living in the Shadow of China's Economic Dominance*, Washington D.C.: Institute of International Economics, 2011.

will be very much similar to that of America of the 1970s and the UK of the 1870s. The role of RMB as one of the major reserve currencies in the world arrives much earlier and faster than we have ever imagined.

Of course, the argument presented in this book is not accepted by all important scholars or experts watching the global economy. Many think otherwise, one of whom is Martin Wolf, a famous columnist of the *Financial Times* based in London and author of a long review of the book, presenting some slightly different viewpoints.[1] It is not that he is completely against this book, but that he believes China as a super country with power politics has many congenital restrictions and defects. America still has advantages in some areas, including technological innovation, military, and the comprehensive research capability represented by universities and research institutes, as well as the advantages in using English and the soft power of the democratic system. These may be difficult obstacles for China to overcome for surpassing America and reaching a dominant position in the world. But I believe this dispute will go on. It is unnecessary for us to go into details for the present.

I will show you the rise of China, however, from another perspective. The evaluation mentioned above is taking the country as a unit. In fact, in an era of economic globalization, the drive for the whole economy, i.e. the major engine for it, is not the country, but the global cities that are able to take part in the international labor division and supply chain at the world level and go through very complex transnational exchanges, transactions and cooperation. They function as creative centers, information centers and financial centers, and meanwhile take part in the global industrial chain and such activities as R&D, management, logistics, financing, etc. It is these cities that are the engine for economic growth and the most important platform for gathering talents, information and capital. Therefore, the scene depicted in *Eclipse* as mentioned above may also be seen in the future of the global cities.

---

[1] http://www.ft.com/intl/cms/s/2/f1447af8-ef61-11e0-bc88-00144feab49a.html.

Global Institute, a think tank under McKinsey — the most influential advisor and counselor in the world, observed 75 cities that feature the qualifications of "global cities" and are the most dynamic in future economic growth, analyzing the process of rise and chase that may occur from 2010 to 2025.[1] They listed 75 global cities whose total economic growth ranked the highest in the world in 2025, naming them as "The Most Dynamic Cities of 2025," based on a model. Out of the 75 cities, 29 were in Mainland China. It is speculated that there would be only 3 such cities in Europe which would be rated as the most dynamic, competitive, creative and growth impetus in the world. There would only be 13 such cities in America, with the second largest number, only second to Mainland China, where there would be 29. Tokyo was ranked No. 1 in the world in terms of the size of their economy in 2010, but its total growth would be ranked No. 10 in 2025, according to the McKinsey estimate. If we take cities as the platform of integrating economic resources, engines for value creation and the cradle for nurturing emerging industries, you may as well foresee how the relative economic position of China would change in a period shorter than 15 years.

Some of the 29 cities are very familiar to us, such as Shanghai and Beijing. Some are quite unexpected but would become the top and most competitive cities, such as Shenyang and Chongqing. Of the first 20 most dynamic global cities by 2025, only 7 cities are not in Mainland China, according to this report. Besides, you would see some cities included quite unexpectedly. It is expected to include Shenzhen, which was only a small fishing village 25 years ago and is now a metropolis with a population of 10 million. Wuhan would not be that unexpected, either. Another example is Foshan, a rising star in the Pearl River delta, has grown to a city of 6 million people and an important base for the electrical appliance industry, and it is continuously growing fast. And then there is Dongguan in Guangdong. It is very difficult to imagine that a place prospered by the operations of Taiwan

---

[1] http://www.foreignpolicy.com/articles/2012/08/13/the_most_dynamic_cities_of_2025.

I would like to show China's fast rise by quoting the comparison of several important indicators of China and America, the two super economies, in the past 10 years and the coming 15 years as published in *The Economist* at the end of 2011. *The Economist* employed many fixed targets, not only GDP. There are some simple examples, such as steel output, in which China surpassed America in 1999, 6.6 times that of America in 2011. It is fair to say that this is not important, because America entered the era of the intellectual economy long ago and steel is not an industry that needs further development in America. Take the mobile phone as another example. The mobile phones used in China were more than those in America in 2001, and increased to 3.3 times those of America in 2011.

The year 2010 witnessed immense changes. China surpassed America in several indicators, the main reason being the global financial crisis in 2008 and 2009 and America being first affected. So the economic growth of the whole western world slowed down, while that of China still continued. Many indicators of China surpassed America in 2010, including gross output, total energy consumption, total auto sales, number of technological patents, etc. According to this analysis, China will become the greatest consumption market in the world by 2023, which is not quite far from now. China's fifth generation of leaders, represented by Mr. Xi Jinping, may lead China on its road to steady development, and this significant target may almost be realized within this administration. Presently, the biggest difference between China and America lies in military expenditure. The military expense of China is only around 22% of America's spending. But based on the ratio of the defense expenditure increase rate to GDP of China presently, China's defense expenditure will have exceeded that of the United States by around 2025 according to *The Economist*'s estimate. Just imagine how great the change is to the growth and decline of these two powers. Under the leadership of Xi Jinping and Li Keqiang, China will undergo significant transformation in politics, economy, military and domestic social structure, and there will also be significant change to its role on the world's political

How to Understand the Rise of China

To all intellectual elites of East Asian countries, the most critical intellectual challenge of the 21st century is how to understand the rise of China in a historical context. If the other East Asian countries fail to understand this very well, they will get nowhere in how to face the future. Let me put it in the most macro historical point of view. The rise of China and the emergence of China's development model is a massive historical change for the whole world. In the past 300 years of man's history, there were only four historical events that might be rivaled with this in terms of its huge impact on or guidance to further development of man's history. The first is the industrial revolution in the UK in the 18th century, the second is the French Revolution in 1789, the third is the Great October Socialist Revolution in Russia in 1917, and the fourth is the rise of America at the end of the 19th century and the beginning of the 20th century. The first two of the four events had profound influences on the world order of the 19th century, and the last two shaped the world structure of the 20th century.

We may say that the change of the old world order guided the evolution of the development model of China, but in the future, the rise of China will necessarily require the world order to restructure. The first point in understanding the impact of the rise of China on the world is to have an objective and overall understanding of the China model. So far, in understanding the China model, the social elites of the neighboring countries are still falling behind, catching up and making up misleading information. Why is there such a big understanding gap and knowledge deficiency? One important reason is that it is too easy for us to understand the China Model based on the historical knowledge and cognitive framework that are familiar to us. It is a natural inclination, which, however, keeps us away from a full picture of it. The basis for our understanding is in fact filled with the West-centered fallacies and misunderstandings which we are totally unaware

---

[1] http://www.economist.com/node/21542155.

perspective and vision. The political leaders and social elites of the US go even further in this respect. They always tend to evaluate China with their values and historical conceptions, and take in the information about China in a selective way, which makes it hard for them to understand China in a very objective and balanced way. If we do not change the old thinking based on preconceptions, prejudice and selective cognitions, it is impossible for us to form a truly balanced understanding.

First, we should try to understand it in the context of man's history. China for the past 30 years or the whole second half of the 20th century may be defined this way. Some call it a "miracle," believing it is the fastest continuous economic growth ever in man's history, for it continuously grows at a speed faster than the rise of the "Four Tigers of East Asia," Japan since the Meiji Restoration, America since the Civil War, Germany, and faster than the modernization of the other advanced western industrial countries which rose much earlier. In addition, it is an industrialization process that has ever taken place to the greatest extent in man's history: there has never been any country or society whose industrialization has taken place with such a large scale and in such a wide geographic scope. This is unprecedented and non-repeatable. China has also realized the elimination of poverty at the greatest scale ever in man's history: over 300 million people have broken away from the poverty line as defined by the UN since the reform and opening up. Never have we seen any other emerging industrialized country being capable of the leapfrogging and salutatory advances in the international labor division system in such a short period. In today's international labor division system, China is engaged in both labor-intensive industries and technology-intensive industries, i.e. both at the low end and at the high end. Taiwan or South Korea used to hope that they might form a vertical division with China, but this option has disappeared. China's international labor division is both vertical and parallel. It could be in such productive-labor-intensive industries as making garments and umbrellas or even decorations for Christmas, but meanwhile, it is able to send satellites into orbits in space and help other countries to build the most rival those of any other big brands in the world. So China is engaged in the international labor division at the capital-intensive and technology-intensive levels at the same time while continuing to keep its strength at the labor-intensive level.

China itself is a huge complex economic system, with great differences going on inside. It has integrated into the world economy at an incredible fast speed. China's entry into the WTO provides such an example. In a short 12 years from 2001 to now, China has become the world's largest exporter, surpassing Germany. In terms of the average tariff, China's degree of openness has surpassed most developing countries. Never has any other developing country attracted such massive transnational capital from all over the world. The Chinese enterprises may also take part in transnational financing. China is directly engaged in developing and constructing the communication facilities and infrastructure at a 21st century level. Many found that, after the global financial crisis in 2009, China was playing an unprecedented role as the engine that is driving the world economic recovery, which was played by America in the past. If China did not take this part, the global economic recovery would have further slowed down. This contributes to an objective historical positioning for the rise of China.

We tend to stick to the nominal method of calculating GDP, so the economy of China would seem relatively smaller. If Purchasing Power Parity (PPP) is used to evaluate GDP, China surpassed Germany as early as in 1982 and Japan in 1992,[1] according to the estimate by Angus Maddison, the most authoritative Dutch economist who recently passed away. The economic aggregate of China was 86% of America in 2006. Therefore, its economic aggregate will have surpassed America in three years based on this estimate. China's economy will remain over 2.5 times that of India in 2015. Of course, some will question and challenge these estimates, but more people think they are somewhat conservative, because these estimates were made before the outburst of the global financial tsunami in September 2008,

---

[1] http://www.ggdc.net/maddison/Maddison.htm.

America and the European countries.

How Has China Realized the Unprecedented Rise?

We are going to answer this question first: How has such a fast, large-scale and unprecedented rise become possible? This issue may need to be explained throughout a whole semester. Simply, there are three special conditions: the first one is the political system of China; second, China has exerted its advantage of being "great," and the third is the late-comer advantage.

The first condition is the special advantage brought about by the political system of China. It is believed by many that the three decades from 1949 to the launch of reform and opening up was wasted; it was utterly a dark period. Actually, this perception itself was wrong. It was not sheer waste in this period. On the contrary, China constructed a foundation for the reform and opening up later at a high social cost (of even many lives) during this period. It is essentially impossible for other countries to copy this foundation, if understanding of it is possible. China constructed a modern national system with an especially strong ability for mobilization during these three decades. Such a system never existed in this land in China's history. The ability of mobilization and permeation reached the very bottom of society. And China has established a very strong national consciousness. China has completed a rather thorough socialist revolution, because it made private property ownership, the biggest part being the land capital and industrial capital, collectivized. These massive collective assets, most of which are state-owned, became the capital for China's fast growth in the past 30 years. Many other countries did not go through this historical approach, so it was quite difficult for them to have this historical condition.

Second, China has exerted its advantage of being "great." In the course of "Political and Economic Changes of China" lecture provided by me to the graduates, I asked them to keep three points in mind in understanding the Mainland: first, China is very great; second, China is very very great; third, greatness can be changed into great advantages. First, China may fully realize the large-scale economy and exert its magnet effect. It is impossible to establish and develop many critical core industries without large scale. It is impossible for South Korea to build the space industry, and it is impossible for Taiwan to build an industrial system for high-speed railways, because they do not have enough big market and/or scale. Strictly speaking, there are only two aviation groups in the world so far: Boeing and Airbus, and it is only possible for Airbus to compete with Boeing by integrating the resources, talents and markets of all the countries in Europe. And then it is most possible for China to become the origin of a third aviation group. If the huge potential is presented, it will produce a huge magnet effect.

All transnational companies in the world have tried their best to enter China. It is not only CEOs that would ask about the "greater China strategy," but also the trustees of the Top 50 universities in America: what greater China strategy does this university have? As a president, you must give a proper answer; if you fail to answer it well, it means that you do not have a forward-looking plan for the university in the 21st century. It is the same with the CEOs of Fortune 500 companies. Therefore, China would be able to set many special conditions on all foreign investments in China, which the transnational companies would otherwise not generally easily accept. For example, General Motors established a new R&D center in Shanghai when it entered China, but GM would not listen to any other country which asks it to "establish a R&D center here," because they do not have the bargaining chips. China has the large scale, so it has a complete technology system and industry system. China has all the necessary knowledge and technological systems it needs for sending a man-made satellite into space. In addition, the 30-year independence has forced China to build a complete system, which may include different levels, some close to the international top level, and some still very backward. But that's all right, because it will be very fast to chase, learn, emulate and improve, either in terms of aircraft carriers or stealth fighters, once such a system is in existence.

Effect," or the "Wild Goose Queue Theory" quite often, which meant that in a vertical system of labor division, Japan was the bellwether which was followed by the "Four Tigers of East Asia," and then the ASEAN, or the emerging industrial countries in the second echelon. But the scale of China is so great that it is possible to produce the "Wild Goose Queue Effect" within itself, meaning that the vertical labor division could be realized internally. It also means that there could be several levels of its growth drive, from coastal areas to Central China, to the west of China, and then to the greater western areas of China, because there are different conditions for development in different areas, including labor cost, land price, etc. There is also different room for improvements in different areas when it comes to productivity.

The third is the late-comer advantage. China has been exerting the later-comer advantage during the past 30 years. The late-comer can also be an early-comer sometimes. There are many merits of being a late-comer. For example, you may learn the successful experiences in the past to avoid the same mistakes and unnecessary attempts, and may make very fast progress, especially when the late-comer is able to emulate and copy others' experiences based on which some improvements can be made. Meanwhile, it is clear that China has carried out the leapfrogging technological update. When it was very difficult for China to have the technology of wired land-phones, it was at the same point of entering the areas of wireless communication and digital communication. Similarly, China may fall behind South Korea and Western Europe in the third-generation communications technology, but it has begun its plans for the fourth and fifth generations of mobile communication. This is what we mean by leapfrogging technological update. Moreover, the timing of reform and opening up of China has made it the biggest beneficiary of globalization. The global economy advanced rapidly in production, product marketing, financial integration, etc. Globalization has sped up in the past 30 years when transnational companies carried out their global production layouts and the restrictions to the flow of transnational capital were removed one after another. Of course, there were customs clearance, container transportation, digital communications, more open capital market, etc. All these conditions have been available in the past 30 years, so China has seized this historical opportunity and exerted the late-comer advantage.

How to Understand the Political and Economic Systems of China

Up to now, the economic system of China is still the socialist market economy, or the market-oriented socialist economic system, which is also the Chinese government's official definition of China's economic system. We should take a serious attitude toward this definition, rather than take it as a propaganda or advertisement, because this definition provides the authentic description of some very important characteristics of this system. On the one hand, in this system, the market mechanism is employed to adjust the supply and demand of raw materials of most commodities and the labor market, to realize price-guided resource distribution. In this respect, this system fully exerts the positive function of the market mechanism in promoting the efficiency of the whole economic system. On the other hand, in terms of ownership, this economic system includes several ownerships, which compete and coexist with each other, seeking mutual growth and guidance. The ownerships could be state-owned, collective, private, or foreign. State-owned enterprises still dominate the mainstay and core sectors of the whole economic system of China. If you see the list of public companies in Shanghai, you'll find that the Top 20 or 30 are all state-owned, including the sectors of banking, energy, transportation, communication, petrochemical and steel.

Up to now, China still holds that the rural land is collectively owned by peasants. The CPC will not carry out full privatization rashly, because privatization will make peasants lose their land and incur drastic changes in the rural social structure, with land annexation and peasants being displaced. There were examples in China's history. Therefore, the CPC does not think

China. The elites of the CPC leaders have been trying continuously to overcome the problem of social imbalance that would appear in the process of development, about whose progress different people may hold their own views. But the motivation for self-correction and responding to social demand still exists. This regime is making incessant efforts to pursue balanced development, including wide coverage with a social security system, so as to resolve the conflicts between the urban and rural areas, between different regions, between labor and capital, and between development and the environment through a fiscal transfer payment as much as possible. You will find that some measures are taken for the first time in history if viewed from the perspective of China's history, including the cancellation of all agricultural taxes, and subsidies provided to rural medical treatment and elementary education both by the central government and local governments. This has been an unprecedented great change in China throughout 3000 years.

The most prominent design of the political system of China is the one-party rule. It seems that this system is incompatible with the world trend, but our observation should be focused on how the one-party rule maintains the political stability and governance capability. There are several interesting points. One is that this system solves the problems of succession crisis and individual dictatorship. Generally, it is very difficult for the one-party rule or the authoritarian regime to cross these two thresholds. China, at least after Mao Zedong, established some systems to overcome these two problems: one is the tenure system, and the other is the collective leadership. The Sixteenth and the Eighteenth National Congresses of the CPC have respectively displayed the actual operation of the tenure system and the succession system. The system of establishing CPC standing committees at different levels also solves the problem of individual dictatorship by implementing the collective leadership. Therefore, the CPC Standing Committee of the Political Bureau of China is like a powerful president, whose role, of course, is played by the nine members collectively. Each member has their own duties, but the most important decisions must be

This system is improving its governing capabilities continuously in order to adapt to the fast changing social environment. The most important mission shouldered by the communist party is to provide the mechanism for talent selection and internal competition, enabling those with certain qualifications and capabilities to undertake more important responsibilities step by step in this system. Moreover, this system also encourages local governments to stay innovative in public governance. The central government plays the role of central planning, because it has the huge mechanism of coordination and counterbalance, including the system of the PLA Military Region and the system of Branches of the People's Bank of China. The central government controls the fundamental resources of energy, transportation, communications and land, as well as the propaganda agencies and personnel appointments. These are critical agencies of the central government employed to control local governments. But in another respect, it seems that it is the federal system that is implemented in China, because the provincial governments are more powerful than the states of America in some areas. This decentralization system has no constitutional basis, but it reflects some characteristics of federalism in actual operation. The result is that local governments may carry out various experimental innovations based on the reality of the specific area. Therefore, the fierce regional competition within the Mainland, if any, would be the competition for resources, talents and funds between provinces, and even counties. For example, Kunshan, under the administration of Suzhou municipality, has changed rapidly from a village to an important town for hi-tech industry. And the cities close to it want to be another Kunshan by emulating its model. This system also has enough incentives for local governments to become stakeholders, so local governments are like corporate groups who are capable of mobilizing and planning all kinds of resources in their own jurisdictions, and provincial governors resemble the CEOs of the corporate groups.

The biggest challenge this political system faces is to select qualified talents and weed out the unqualified and to make sure that proper persons the Organization Department of the CPC is the HR department with the toughest tasks in the world in this sense. The challenge of management faced by this HR department is far greater than that faced by any of the largest global corporations, such as GE or US Software Group. In fact, the challenge is also far greater than that of the official system we used to think the most colossal, such as the US Department of Defense. It is even fair to say that, to some extent, the functions of talent selection, regular weeding out and competitive selection within the CPC are very much like the HR management of the US Department of Defense. Why is that? This is a closed system, in which cadres at all levels get promoted internally. If one wants to be the Commander-in-Chief, it is impossible for him to get the position as an outsider of the system; one has to start from the Second Lieutenant and get promoted rank by rank within the system. But not every Second Lieutenant has the opportunity to be promoted to Captain, and not every Captain has the opportunity to be promoted to Major. On the very top of the pyramid there are only seven people. There is also such a pyramid structure in the US army.

What type of mechanisms should be employed to administer and select talents? This is a colossal and formidable task, which has never been faced by any other human societies. When you pass Chang'an Street in Beijing, you will find a secluded building. This is the head office of the "HR department": Organization Department of the CPC Central Committee, whose subordinate departments take care of the organization of 13 million Party cadres, from selection, to training and evaluation, and to promotion or weeding out. Though the political system of China does not include the democratic mechanism defined by the West, the socialist democratic mechanism is not merely superficial; it has the practical functions. The most important function is the selection and evaluation of cadres. In the Mainland, many local organization departments entrust public-opinion institutions every year to conduct public opinion polls of all government institutions, to find out whether the public are satisfied with these institutions or not. Those lagging behind will receive warnings, and for those lagging behind again the many units announce the qualified candidates before internal promotion, and all members of the unit will be asked to vote for these candidates anonymously. These examples show that China has its counterbalance and accountability mechanism through its own exploration.

In many cities in the Mainland, especially the comparatively developed cities in the coastal areas, the citizens have expressed higher demands for taking part in politics. The local governments all establish a consultation mechanism to include the opinions of stakeholders. Significant constructions must be included in the consultation mechanism for citizens or interested groups to air their opinions. Local governments may sometimes be so flexible in working out and implementing measures that fit the local reality that they may not follow the policies and requirements of the central government. What's more, the constant public protests carried out in the Mainland in recent years may not necessarily mean political instability; the frequent occurrence of these events also means that this system also allows for the release of social conflicts and pressure. The upper level actually acquiesces to tantrums, whistle-blowing, petitioning and even protests. Collective protests are the most possible means of self-protection to be adopted by the local public when they cannot tolerate something any longer, in order to expose problems, so the higher-level authority will delegate someone to investigate into the matter, and defects are revealed in many cases. Presently, the CPC central leaders impose very strict requirements on how to deal with massive public protests, and the top leader of the local government has to deal with those events in person, and rash use of force is strictly forbidden.

These are the measures China has taken to face a transitional society that changes quickly. China actually keeps adjusting many internal mechanisms to resolve social conflicts, to allow for certain mechanisms for expressing social benefits and forms the counterbalance against cadres, or the "accountability mechanism." It has recently imported the accountability audit. After any cadre at the level above deputy department director retires from the position, all the funds and budgets he or she handled within term of

Problems are often found during this process. This mechanism shows the remarkable dated adjustment of policies in the Mainland.

Then, we should learn that it is impossible for the one-party system to be born without its cultural background, which is the most familiar to the world of Confucian culture, because this system is essentially established on the basis of "government for the people" rather than "government by the people." The basis of the regime is very abstract, understandable but inexpressible. It is called "aspiration of the people," but not votes. The concept of "aspiration of the people" itself is a core concept in the traditional political legitimacy of China. The Confucian idea of "people-oriented government" is essentially a kind of elite politics, which is intended to achieve the objective of "government for people" or "people-oriented government." It may be confronted with a great variety of obstacles, even irresolvable problems. But the construction of the political legitimacy of this political system has its basis for expounding construction.

Due to this fact, western scholars are very confused about the political system of China, based on which China is rising in all aspects through such a fast industrialization. According to their political experience, how could the "government by people" be possible without the "government for people?" But the scholars in the Mainland may ask you this question: the Philippines have the "government by people," but does it have the "government for people?" So these two cannot be treated equally. They observed China's capabilities of planning the Beijing Olympics, providing rescues and reliefs after the Sichuan Earthquake, and responding to the global financial tsunami in a balanced way. They found that even their governments are not qualified to respond to these events and crises and meet those challenges in such a fast and effective way. So Tom Friedman, a famous columnist with the *New York Times* and author of a bestseller, *The World Is Flat*, includes a chapter titled "Let's be China for a day" in his the US system. He's much more worried that America will fail to help the country face the 21st century challenges efficiently if the internal frictions continue. He is particularly concerned that it is necessary for the US to develop a green economy and plan a big research budget for renewable energies. But he also finds that the interest groups representative of the petrol and energy industries are so big that they may manipulate the legislation of this category in the Congress. Friedman muses on how good it would be to have the Chinese system, but for one day only, so as to do so much for the 21st century by fiat in one day, and then be America again the next day. This is of course a dream, but he expounded the difference between the two systems in a dramatic way.

To Interpret the Rise of China in a Macro-History

The rise of China must be interpreted in a macro-history, without which it is impossible to get a clear picture. That's why I use the word of "rise" instead of "upstart." Actually, it should be "re-rise" instead of "upstart," because during the reign of Emperor Qianlong of the Qing Dynasty, China's GDP (PPP), took up more than 1/4 of the world's total, according to Angus Maddison's calculation method. China's GDP declined to the lowest in history in the beginning of the 20th century, only 3% of the world's total and fell behind for good. One reason might be that the other countries advanced too fast, especially Western Europe and the US. From this point of view, China is now only recovering its quota in the world, and restoring its position in East Asia. What we have seen today is only the prelude of the process of restoration. More importantly, China is reshaping the world order. But this is not the first time for it to shape the world order. In history, it used to be an important actor and participator in shaping the world order. It may not be well known to all that China's trade accounted for over 50% of the world's total in the Ming Dynasty 600 years ago. The silver plundered by

---

[1] Thomas Friedman, *Hot, Flat, and Crowded: Why We Need a Green Revolution and How It Can Renew America*, Farrar, Straus and Giroux, 2008.

government of the Ming Dynasty enjoyed massive trade surplus, major exports including tea, silk, china and traditional Chinese medicines. The domestic manufacturing industry was also very developed, so it needed little import.

In the end, based on the macro-history, we should understand the "re-rise" of China in a more macro perspective. The rise of China is a part of the "all-round rise of the non-western world," the big story itself being the main plotline of the historical change of the world from the last four decades of the 20th century to the beginning of the 21st century. All the economic stagnations of Europe and the long declination of Japan are actually included in this context of macro-history. It is fair to say that man's history has entered a new period, in which the traditional "North-South Relationship" begins to have fundamental changes. Generally, the "North" we mention refers to advanced industrial countries, though they are not all in the northern hemisphere, but most of them are, the few exceptions include Australia and New Zealand. The colonized or underdeveloped countries are basically in the southern hemisphere, especially in Africa and South Asia, as well as Latin America. What is the traditional "North-South Relationship?" It means that the industrialized countries in the northern hemisphere always have the advantages in technology, military and banking. They control the world affairs, and define various game rules for the whole world based on their benefits. Besides, they have maintained their lasting advantages by all means, sometimes free trade, sometimes colonial plunder. They enjoy much higher living standards than these southern countries. The wealth and the means of creating wealth of the whole world are centralized in them. The most typical is that they export industrial products at very high prices, exchanging for industrial raw materials, agricultural products and energy at very cheap prices. The Central American countries have to export tons of bananas for only one fridge. Some scholars call this the asymmetric exchange, or unfair exchange, between the North and the South.

This kind of asymmetric relationship cannot endure, because backward countries may come to learn, emulate and catch up. Many non-western colonized or caught in civil wars. Japan was the forerunner in this sense, and then it was the "Four Asian Tigers," and then many more emerging economies, which contributed to the new historical era of all-round rise of non-western countries. These late-comers have joined in the process of rapid industrialization; they will enter the field of high technology the northern countries were best at in the past, and will challenge the advanced industries dominated and monopolized by northern countries in the past. At that time, the exchanges between the North and the South will be fundamentally changed. This change will be very simple. It could be put in a way as simple as: the prices of anything that China and India are capable of producing will all rise. The prices of anything that China and India, the list of which may of course include Brazil, Mexico, Indonesia, and so on, are capable of manufacturing will go down continuously. It is a very simple scenario. Salmon became more and more expensive than they were five years ago, because it is very difficult to increase the total output of salmon. But the demand of China and India will grow very fast. It may cost you less than USD 100 to buy a DVD player at the night fair. A few years later, it is very easy for one to get an iPhone at less than RMB 1,000. This may show the fundamental shift in the "North-South Relationship."

We are facing a great transformation that did not occur in the past 300 years: the focus of world is shifting rapidly to the non-western world. What is "the West?" In a traditional sense, the West refers to Western Europe, and the US, Canada, New Zealand and Australia. Of course some people also include Japan in the West, which is another definition; the traditional definition of the West did not include Japan. But Japan always believes itself as one of the members of the Western Group. The redistribution of the wealth and power of the whole world is accelerated, which only means that the non-western world is recovering their roles on the world's economic and political stage. That's all. I mentioned previously that China used to be a significant member in the world economy. It may not be noticed that Arabia also used to be like this, and it was the same case with India — India was a very important part of the world economy at least before it was relegated world economy encountered such earthshaking changes, which shows that the world we used to be familiar with would not endure forever. It has actually changed drastically, which has been spotted by some acute observers of the countries in the West. Before the breakout of the subprime crisis, Fareed Zakaria, the former Chief Editor of *Newsweek* published a book titled *The Post-American World* in 2008,[1] which discusses this great historical transformation and trend. He described that the current transition was the second most important structural shift of man's history in the past 500 years. The first was the rise of the western world, mainly referring to Western Europe; the second was the rise of the US; and the third one was the rise of the non-western world. This was exactly what he said. The dean of the Lee Kuan Yew School of Public Policy in Singapore, Kishore Mahbubani, an Indian Singaporean, wrote a book titled *The New Asian Hemisphere*.[2] Historians referred to the rise of the US as the rise of the "western hemisphere," meaning the rise of the western hemisphere led by the US. So he referred to Asia as the "Asian hemisphere" by borrowing this concept, believing it was going to be a new important role on the world political and economic stage. It is also mentioned in this book that China, India, the Muslim countries and many other nations used to have major roles in the world in history. Without the Arabians who brought the classics on astronomy, medicine and mathematics and the classics of ancient Greece to Europe, there would not have been the Renaissance in Europe.

Percentage of Global GDP (last 500 years)

The exquisite historical estimate made by Maddison is an estimate of the size of each economy for different historical phases. A large quantity of materials and different methods were needed for this estimate. The following figure (see Fig. 1) only displays a part of his data. Let's have a

---

[1] Fareed Zakaria, *The Post-American World*, W.W. Norton & Company, 2008.
[2] Kishore Mahbubani, *The New Asian Hemisphere: The Irresistible Shift of Global Power to the East*, Public Affairs, 2009.

of this period, i.e. the end of Emperor Qianlong's reign and the beginning of Emperor Jiaqing's reign, until when China's GDP always accounted for over 1/4 of the world's total. Sometimes it was smaller maybe because of war affairs and sometimes bigger, but it was basically around 1/4. India was also a very big economy in the world. Then it was colonized by the UK and became a plunder of the UK through the East India Company. America's economy surged after the Civil War at the end of the 19th century, and reached its climax after WWII. But we should remember that the total population of North American and Europe accounted for only a little more than 1/10 of the world's total, but they used to enjoy over half of the world's productivity. Frankly speaking, it was an exception in man's history, not a normal case. It is impossible for this exception to last long. The reason is that once the other countries regain their independence and break away from other countries' control, they will be able to begin to develop, emulate and catch up. Some have succeeded, some not, but the great trend is still there. It is quite impossible for them to be forever far ahead in technological development.

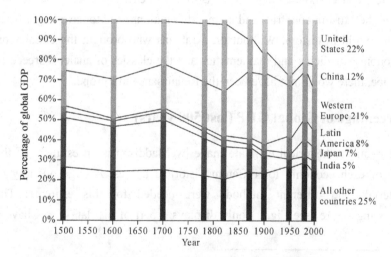

Fig. 1　Percentage of global GDP (last 500 years)

Source: Angus Maddison, University of Groningen.

inelegant group good at plagiary and emulation. How were they able to catch up with Western Europe? But America had been fully geared to bridge the gap since the end of the Civil War in the 1860s. The process of catching up was actually a process of copying for America. Anything invented in Europe would find their counterfeits or reproductions in New York and Boston after three months. In this period of history, America would of course not pay any respect for the European intellectual properties. America is leading now, but it turns out to be requiring the countries falling behind to strictly follow the rules of intellectual property and takes it as important for trade negotiation. Each country shares the experiences of such catching up. Let's say the other way round. China did not charge any other countries a royalty for many important inventions, such as the movable printing, gunpowder and compass, because there was no rule or law on patents available at that time.

Multiple Modernities of the Rise of the Non-Western World

Angus Maddison made an estimate about the future based on this model. This estimate corresponds to the book *Eclipse* I mentioned previously, although his focus was placed on GDP while Subramanian's focus was on the distribution of world economic activities, especially trade and investment. They stressed different aspects, but shared largely the same view on the overall trend. According to the estimate of this model, by 2030, Western Europe's GDP will have declined to the world's by 12%, from over 1/4, their peak, before the oil crisis. Comparatively, America slowed down at a slower pace, because America will continue to have new immigrants and its population will be increasing, and its technology is superior to Europe in an overall sense. According to many scholars' views now on this estimate, the estimate of China's GDP should be somewhat conservative. Most importantly, the GDP of the western world accounted for around 51% before the oil crisis and over 56% immediately after WW II. It was not strange that the western powers including the US, UK and France came to restructure the international system, because they used to stand in the unrivaled leading and dominating positions. But in an overall sense, the GDP of the western world will be less than 1/3 of the world's total by 2030, while the non-western world in a broad sense will have exceeded 2/3. At that time, the world will by no means remain the one we were familiar with. Tremendous changes will occur in history. Actually, such changes have already appeared, but in a way that it is still an ongoing process with the finale not yet firmly determined (See Fig. 2).

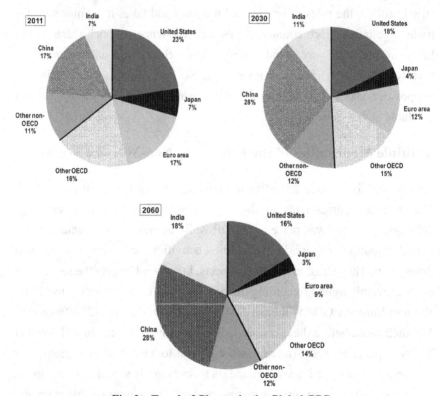

Fig. 2   Trend of Change in the Global GDP
Source: Johansson, A., et al., Looking to 2060: Long-Term Global Growth Prospects: A Going for Growth Report, OECD Economic Policy Papers, No. 3, 2012.

The redistribution of global productivity and wealth will inevitably bring about the change in the power structure and ideological structure. Prof.

published a review in the bi-monthly *National Interest* in 2008. They reminded the readers of what the leaders of the western world thought about the world order and what type of rules and systems should be adopted to manage global affairs. This is a kind of West-centered thinking. Little study was done before on what the world was probably going to be when such West-centered thinking was gradually weeded out or forced to change. They thought the options for non-western countries were not limited to either getting integrated into the West-dominated international system or challenging the existing world order. Instead, non-western countries may also choose to detour around the system constructed by the West and construct another set of rules for international exchange based on different world outlook and values, and then leaving the international standards constructed by western countries aside.

In the future development, these three changes will all occur. Non-western countries will accept international rules on exchange and multilateral system selectively, but they will desire to reform. Meanwhile, they will detour around the system constructed by the West and construct cooperation systems and multilateral organizations themselves. It is also necessary for western countries to give in and make some adjustments. For example, nobody takes G8 that seriously since 2008, because it has been replaced by G20. Why is there G20? Why did G8 (G7 in fact) have to give up the stage? The reason lies in the inevitable trend.

In addition, the BRICS is being substantiated. The BRICS (including South Africa) has started to challenge the West-dominated world order, and has established a set of cooperation mechanisms separate from the existing West-dominated cooperation systems and standards. Of course, it is still burgeoning, but already features some momentum.

The rise of China drives the all-round rise of the western world, changing the conditions on the exchanges between industrial products and raw materials and accelerating the redistribution of world wealth. Of course, this redistribution does not mean that all western countries are declining. There are still lucky ones, such as Canada and Australia, which feature resources of forests, iron mines and oil shale, so they may benefit from the all-round rise of the non-western world.

But from the perspective of core values, it is more important that the historical structure of unitary modernity we used to know is disappearing. In that structure, the West represented the most advanced, while the other countries could do nothing but emulating and approaching them, so the coordinate of the advanced and the backward was very clear. It is almost certain that the 21st century is characterized with multiple modernities. Countries with different historical and cultural backgrounds may choose different paths to modernity, and there is modernity, either common or unique, embodied in the form and organizing principles of their mature and stable modern societies. Not all countries would become the US or Germany. In fact, Japan did not follow the way of the US or Germany. Japan is a highly modernized country, but it has different social and political operation models from the US and Europe. But people sometimes neglect the differences and instead focus on what they have in common, imposing historical structure of unitary modernity on the comparisons.

The tremendous change of Africa in the past 10 years was never seen since Africa's independence. It is all because these countries have been speeding up developing relationships with China, India and Brazil, forming new relationships in economic exchange and mutual benefits. The trade amount between China and Africa reached USD 160 billion in 2011, accounting for 18% of the total foreign trade amount of Africa. On the reverse, China relies more on Africa's energies. China also started various investments, amounting to USD 40 billion by the end of 2010. During this period, many financial institutions of China played very important roles. In the past decade, 2001–2010, the Export-Import Bank of China granted a variety of loans to Africa, short-term or long-term, the total amount of financing reaching USD 67.2 billion. The World Bank, the institution providing preferential loans to the most important developing countries in the world, financed only over USD 50 billion during this period. Hence you may see the change. China has exempted the USD 30 billion loan to 35 poor

Africa and begins to play a role there; this is the China Development Bank. With total assets exceeding the sum of the assets of the World Bank and Asian Development Bank, it is going to provide financing to Africa through the medium-and-small-sized Chinese enterprises which work with Africa. You will find the same situation in Latin America.

Therefore, in this sense, China's development path will influence the future of man. It has shocked the mainstream economic circles in the West, and shaken the power of discourse of the old international development institutions, including the International Monetary Fund and World Bank, on development and governance. In the past, these institutions thought they knew how to guide Africa, Latin America and Asia how to develop, how to carry out political reforms and how to formulate economic development strategies. But their old dominating position has been greatly changed. It is also because of this change that it was possible for Mr. Justin Yifu Lin to perform as Vice President of World Bank.

It is possible for the socialist market economy of China to have a standing in the ideological domain of the whole world. This trend is not that remarkable in East Asia, but it is in Africa, Latin America and South Asia. It is possible to create a third path besides the American capitalism and the democratic socialism of Western Europe (the welfare state). It will force the political elites of all the countries of the Third World to rethink about how to balance due procedures, maintain the government's governance capability and reap the best results out of development, and what kind of efficient policies, arrangements and strategies can be adopted for balance between them.

Recently, the most influential magazine *Economist* has also realized this challenge, although it is reluctant to adopt the term of "socialist market economy," the official term used by the Chinese government and instead gives it another term, "State Capitalism," as far as the system of China is concerned. But it has indeed noticed such change, hence airing its worry that the welfare state model of Western Europe is facing collapse, the American capitalism is challenged, and State Capitalism has become a mainstream countries.

Therefore, if I am asked to make any assumption and description of the new coordinate of the 21st century world economy, I would say that the BRICS will become the leader and spokesman of the non-western world and replace the power of discourse in global issues step by step, and G7 will lose the dominating power in formulating multilateral systems and standards over time. It is of course not tomorrow that we will see a completely new result, but the process is ongoing and there will be dramatic changes in the coming 10 or 15 years, or even a shorter period. It is foreseeable that the US and Europe, except Germany which is able to maintain competitive, is becoming more stressful at the challenges in the economy due to the relative decline of their positions. And the trade protectionism will arise again. However, emerging economies will come to play a major role in maintaining global trade. 20 years ago, it was a completely reversed situation.

I also predict that the emerging economies will rely on each other more and more, establishing closer partnerships with each other in trade, finance, energy and the environment. At the recent summit of the BRICS held in New Delhi, an agreement was reached that they would found a development bank of their own, which, once established, will definitely threaten the present position of the World Bank. Meanwhile, I also believe that the USD will sooner or later lose its dominating position as the world reserve currency, but it is almost impossible for a super-sovereign currency to replace the USD for good in a short period of time. Then there will be a pluralistic situation in which several currencies are used for settlement and regionalization in international trade. For example, in a specific region, a currency will be the major currency for capital market operations and settlement. Of course, the Euro will have its position. It also becomes increasingly possible for RMB to be a major currency in East Asia.

That's why I mentioned just now that western countries have to accept G20. The reason is simple. They need the emerging economies to undertake new responsibilities. They hope that they could increase spending and expand consumption to promote the export from western countries. They

Fund, the World Bank and other global financial or fiscal bail-outs by utilizing their savings and foreign currency reserves. They also hope that the countries with abundant foreign currency reserves would continue to buy the national debt of the US and drive lower the long-term interest rates. It is natural for western countries to spare a place for the emerging economies as long as they want them to contribute to their development.

We are now very much concerned with how the standards in many areas, except the economy, could be defined. For example, as to the global warming, one of the most important concerns in the world, how shall we reach a new protocol as the post *Kyoto Protocol*? The game rules were dominated by Western Europe in the past. The US is greatly against this conception and is not willing to accept any global agreement on compulsory reduction of greenhouse gas emissions, and has become a big power that is very passive on this issue. So Europe becomes the leader. Europe actually puts their benefits in the first place in many aspects in designing the rules. This leadership was challenged as early as 2009, wherefrom it is impossible for it to recover this position — It becomes inevitable for them to negotiate with and face the requirements of the non-western group, represented by East Asia, India and Brazil, on the covenant on global climate change. Hence, it can be noted that the world is changing drastically. Although it is still far away to say that BRICS is a political group that is closely united, for there are many conflicts between them, especially between China and India. However, it can be seen from the declaration made at the BRICS summit held in New Delhi in March 2012 that they have actually found some common understanding and viewpoints on some global issues, because it is still a group that is energetically catching up and still relatively falling behind after all. They proposed to establish an international currency and financial system that is fair, just, compatible and orderly. What does this claim mean? It means that the existing international financial system is unfair, unjust, incompatible and disorderly. But they have expressed their dissatisfaction with the existing system in a positive way. Why is that it is always an American or a European to perform as the president of the economic power distribution has changed so tremendously, if the western countries do not let go of these management institutions and multilateral systems become looser in their hands, non-western countries will tinker around on their own and finally make it; the latter believe that they have to rely on reform in themselves if they cannot rely on western countries' initiatives of reform, and the internal reform will create greater impact.

Let's see the new economic order of East Asia. I think the situation is also very clear. China and India will become the engines driving the economic growth of East Asia for a very long time in the future. The East Asian countries on the whole will reduce their dependence on the American and European markets, and reinforce their economic cooperation with other emerging economies, including Latin America, the Middle East and Africa. China will become the leader promoting the regional economic integration of East Asia. It is quite impossible for Japan to become such a leader. Even though the East Asian countries would not form an official and tangible currency alliance, it is still possible for them to form a currency alliance in a certain form, including publishing their own currencies and currency policies, as well as holding more national debts of each other. RMB will become an increasingly important settlement currency in this region and become the major invoicing currency in the Asian bond market.

It is not really noticed by the Taiwan people that the historical success of Taiwan could be attributed to its oceanic location that exerted its advantages. There is nothing wrong here. There were many wars and tough trading obstacles on the land in a period in history, while the paths on the ocean are the most passable and accessible. But such a change has emerged presently. The Trans-Asia Railway will become an accelerator in the regional economic integration of Asia. Not long after, there will be expressways and even high-speed railways linking Kunming directly to Singapore. If it is possible for North Korea to reform at an accelerated speed, it is definitely imaginable to have high-speed railways running from Changchun and along the boundary all the way to Pyongyang, and then Seoul. Today, it only takes no more than 15 days to transport a container from Chongqing, an

Hamburg in Germany, without customs clearance on the way, because all the countries along the route have signed an agreement so as to deliver a sealed container directly to Europe. So it only takes over 21 days to deliver the same container from Shanghai to Amsterdam. Many new changes are worth our concern. Thus, this old silk-road across Central Asia will be reconstructed through a modern transportation system. These could all be included in the new order of East Asia we are going to face.

Conclusion

The rise of China is one of the most important transforming forces shocking the present world structure, and will be one of the forces leading the restructuring of world order in the 21st century. In this sense, China's model of development will influence the restructuring of world order, and China's path of development will influence the future of the human community. The remarkable achievements that have been made through China's development model have shocked the mainstream economic circles in the West, and shaken the power of discourse of the old international development institutions on development and governance. The China model provides a broader space for thinking and choice-making of many Third-world countries while they are thinking about how to strike a balance between social justness, sustainable development and the Libreville competition efficiency. The practical experience of China's political model is also very outstanding in guiding the communities to aspire for best public choices; in particular, it opens up another path to "political legitimacy" other than the representative democracy system of the West. In man's history of development, the rise of China and the emergence of China's development will speed up the deconstruction of the framework of unitary modernity and the establishment of the framework of multiple modernities. In the future, the history of the West will no longer be the only reference structure, nor is it fair to define the "advance" or "backwardness" of a civilization with simplistic and formal indicators. In a world with multi-power, there is no a through practice and time in different social environments and different historical conditions before they obtain legitimacy in a particular space and period. No country will obtain a superior position in political civilization merely by putting on the overcoat of "representative democracy," it is not only necessary for the modern representative democracy system of the West to guarantee such core factors as free rights guarantee, political participation, power counterbalance and fair competition, but it must also highly satisfy the citizens' expectations of the most fundamental functions of the state and government, including securing personal safety, improving personal development, maintaining social justice, and maintaining the existence and development of the nation and the country, only based on which the representative democracy is able to compete with the China model in the ideological sphere.

The all-round rise of the non-western world also means that the human community will be facing two possible historical development situations at the same time. On the one hand, the world order may enter a long period of disintegration and restructuring, during which it is hard to avoid disorder and chaos to some degree and many public governance issues at the global level may be put aside almost for good. On the other hand, we may be welcoming the arrival of a more just world order: an international economic exchange model better reflecting the principle of equality and reciprocity, and a global sphere for public discussion showing more respect for cultural and religious pluralism; a world order that serves the need of sustainable development of the majority on the earth and a world order that better reflects the philosophy that all nations go through thick and thin together and enjoy harmony in diversity.

3

When China Takes Over the World

Klas Eklund

Klas Eklund

He completed a BA degree in economics from the Stockholm School of Economics, where he later completed a Licentiate degree. He also has a degree in economic history and Russian from the University of Stockholm.

From 1982 until 1990, he was employed in the Swedish Ministry of Finance, where he finally held the position of deputy under-secretary of state, and in the Prime Minister's Office, where he was an economic policy adviser and speechwriter to the PM. He was one of the closest collaborators of Kjell-Olof Feldt, the then Minister of Finance, and was seen as one of the leading modernisers of the Swedish Social Democratic party. He has chaired several government commissions, including "The productivity commission" and "The commission to enhance the efficiency of the public sector". Eklund was also the secretary of a joint effort from the labour movement to write a strategic vision of the future beyond the welfare state (1989). He has served as an economic policy adviser to the European Commission, and participated in an international expert group which in 2009 published a plan for China's climate policy.

From 1994 to 2007 he was the chief economist of Skandinaviska Enskilda Banken, one of the largest banks in Scandinavia. Since 2007, he is of economics, University of Lund. He is on a number of boards including the International Institute of Industrial and Environmental Economics at the University of Lund, and Mistra, a government-funded foundation for environmental research. In 2011, he was appointed member of the Swedish government's "Commission for the Future", chaired by the Prime Minister.

In 2010, Klas Eklund received the first Jacob Palmstierna award for economic writing. In 2012 he was ranked the most influential person in Sweden as regards sustainability issues. He was also selected as a member of the Royal Swedish Academy of Engineering Sciences IVA.

His many publications include the textbook Vår ekonomi. En introduktion till samhällsekonomin ("Our Economy: An Introduction to Economics"), which so far has been published in 13 Swedish editions and is translated into both Russian and Chinese. He has published some 900 articles in different magazines and newspapers. He has written books on taxes, globalisation and growth. Klas Eklund has also published a book on climate change, "Vårt klimat" ("Our Climate", 2009), a biography of former Swedish PM Olof Palme (2010, as part of a big history project with biographies of all Swedish Prime Ministers since 1900), and a book about China's economic and political development (2011). His most recent book is about innovation policy ("A framework for innovation policy", 2012). Apart from economic and political publications, he has written the political thriller Läckan ("The Leak", 1990) which was made into a TV series, broadcast on Swedish national television in 1994, now available on DVD.

extent, and furthermore it lacks the similar tradition of using force to spread its ideology around the world.

Western diplomats often criticize China's diplomatic policy, claiming that China has not assumed the global responsibility that people are entitled to ask from a superpower; however, China has reached great heights in the last few decades, and especially considering the fact that it started as a poor and isolated Maoist country without much international influence, it has received more criticism. Today Hong Kong and Macao have returned to China peacefully, and the prospect of a peaceful reunification with Taiwan is even a more optimistic possibility. China has large reserves, is building the biggest business center in world history, and possesses abundant natural resources, bonds and land. China's development model has gained the respect of many developing countries.

From my perspective, China can inevitably become the world's dominant superpower, with its development making an impact all over the world.

Make Progress and a Military Buildup

The development of China's military force has fallen behind its economic development. Two Iraqi Wars in 1991 and 2003 convinced Chinese leaders that their military capacity, their speed, firepower, range, technology, communications and intelligence system lagged far behind those of the USA. Although China has the largest conventional forces with 2 million soldiers, and the country has the ability to expand greatly, in today's battlefields, quantity has no decisive significance. Speed, accuracy and firepower carry more weight. The army therefore is supposed to be professional and to possess high-tech weapon systems.

The huge investment in new weapons and a comprehensive system is a consequence of this. China's military expenditures are multiplying rapidly, despite the fact that it lagged behind those of the USA at the beginning. Since 2000, China's military spending has had a fivefold increase, but that of the USA has doubled. Due to its high starting level, US military spending

GDP, US military spending is much higher than China's.

The rapid growth of China's military spending has narrowed the gap between the two countries, and initial success has been achieved in the country's investment in new weapons systems. What is spectacular is the arrival of the most modern airplanes that can dodge radar as well as the enormous investment made for the building of the first aircraft carrier. New-generation missiles are able to bombard and sink an American aircraft carrier far away from China's coast. China's ambitious space engineering, represented by the 2008 Space Walk and the 2013 Moon Landing project, symbolizes a new generation of the country's military technology. In the March 2011 war in Libya China evacuated local Chinese residents as quickly as it could. More than 30,000 people left by airplane or ship within a few days, which is equivalent to 3 infantry divisions. Only a small number of countries are capable of transporting such a multitude of people from one side of the earth to the other.

All of this makes up a huge military power which is capable of expanding its range of movement and intensifying its political impact.

Outsiders have occasionally felt suspicious about whether the Communist Party of China can control the army in the long run. This suspicion is not without grounds. As army leaders gradually grow more professional, and the establishment of high-tech military armory, the army will deviate more and more every day from the tradition of guerilla set up in Mao's times: Political committee deputies are in power, while soldiers and farmers work and live together.

The relations between the Communist Party and managers, professors and experts in other fields who want to expand freedom of action face a similar challenge. However, because the army has weapons, this relationship is of a different nature. The Communist Party has had conflicts with its army throughout history. For example, Peng Dehuai, the Minister of National Defense, was eradicated due to his disapproval of the Great Leap Forward (1958-1961), an economic and social campaign led by Mao Zedong and aimed to rapidly transform the country from an agrarian economy into a

Likewise, during the "Cultural Revolution" (1966–1976), the army controlled by the "Gang of Four" group administrated the country at first, established a country inside the country, and then was squelched, and the military leader Lin Biao died during the escape in 1971. Therefore, if the Communist Party was desperate to control the army, Communist Party leaders will take the role of the president of Central Army Committee. Nevertheless, the tendency has shown that professionalism is helping the army get rid of daily political control, reducing the sense of belonging to the Communist Party. In order to gain the army's support, Communist Party leaders have no choice but to please the army in a variety of ways.

Peaceful Rise

What is astounding is that China's rapid rise occurs without any huge political or military conflicts. In the past, national leaders' supersedure would have experienced quite a different situation. European powers were at war to gain a dominant position.

China's rapid rise has so far caused such a conflict. Up until now, China's expansion has been primarily in the economy. In politics, people have made efforts to avoid challenging the USA in Latin America — the USA's power area. China is too weak militarily to pose any threat to the USA. China stresses peaceful development and has been expanding its impact in this way. China's slogan is "peaceful rise", and judging from the current conditions, what it says is in accordance with what it does.

In history, China has been relatively peaceful. China's emperors have led China as a cultural and economic center for its small neighboring countries and vassal states, but have not conquered them militarily. Historically, this leading country has been a complacent country, quite different from the USA and another super power. They both have achieved expansion through war and occupation.

It is difficult to predict the future. As China's economic clout is on the rise, political conflict seems inevitable. With the intensification of internal conflicts, nationalistic sentiment is growing. Now it has been argued that China should take diplomatic measures to be tougher on the United States. The United States has a "strategic mistrust" of China, and few people believe that the Chinese will continue to adhere to a peaceful development once it grows to be more powerful.

Faced with the unexpected competition from the Chinese for senior positions, protectionism is rising in some Western countries. Arguments over the RMB exchange rate might be sharpened, and political protests against China's purchasing securities and enterprises may be running high. Likewise, people oppose the expansion of China's leading government-supported enterprises. China would probably hold more capital input for these "go out" enterprises, and thus spark more countermeasures from the USA and the EU. Regional interests will lead to contradiction as well. In Africa and Latin America, the competition for natural resources and resources will be sharpened. The financial burden related to the policy concerning the climate may last for quite a long time.

The United States may choose a head-on approach to cope with one or several issues mentioned above, and China may also choose provocative action. With oil output peaking or stagnant, earth's energy fight could become the spark of conflict. The greatest danger is that one or several such conflicts may lead to an arms race in Southeast Asia.

The situation is not clear, but history has proven that super powers will by no means step down from the stage of history. But precisely the USA has a heinous history, and it has a special knowledge of American civilization — American Exceptionalism. This is a kind of paranoia, more outward-oriented and more aggressive than China's traditional superiority. China thinks itself at least as good as the USA, but to some extent is content with its current role, and does not have the same tradition of sowing the good seed globally as the USA has.

Can China remain unified faced with quite a number of challenges? Multitudes of people argue that when internal conflicts and the tension of international relationship mount, China will move closer to breaking up like the Soviet Union did. This metaphor is inappropriate. The Soviet Union is a young multiracial country of different nationalities established by means of military occupation, so when the leaders of the country failed to cooperate, it was natural for members of the empire to seek independence.

However, China has a much longer history as a unified nation. China is steeped in history, and it was not founded on the basis of military occupation, so ethnic division will not be a threat. 92% of the Chinese are Han people, with the remaining 8% made up of 55 ethnic minorities such as Tibetan, Uyghur, and Mongolian. The largest minority is *Zhuang* which borders on Vietnam. Therefore, there are no ethnic clashes or racial conflicts which would influence China's national unification.

Huge challenges stem from what the government would do to cope with people's growing desire for free speech and anti-corruption. At present, people are not pressing for a multiparty system and Western democracy, but the Communist Party chose to suppress limited discharging resentment. This requires a large-scale social campaign. The Internet provides new possibilities for communication, venting resentment and brief interviews. The Communist Party's overall control over the society has broken down, and the Communist Party has responded to this problem by reinforcing its online control and by strengthening its control over public opinions.

The conflict between government control and the residents' desire to enhance their level of education and open up new channels of communication must be resolved in one way or another. At present this relationship is unstable, and in the long run it would not be conducive to creative performance and economic development. Considering all of the above aspects, the argument that Western democracy would work in China is too simplistic. My personal opinion is that the government will be forced to gradually be more open, and that the Communist Party will have to listen to party. However, the road leading to success is bound to be full of difficulties.

China Becomes No. 1

If China can continue to reform, and if the world can avoid the bloodshed caused by China's rising, China will soon regain its leading position after a period of more than 200 years. There are two reasons. One is its huge population, and the other is that the only country which is capable of challenging China — India is left far behind economically. This has offered a significant opportunity to China. When China goes back to being the leading country in an integrated world, it would influence international community more profoundly than when its economy hit the top of the world.

Economically, this world would be sharply distinct from the one we are accustomed to. I was born in the 1950s, when the American economy was at its peak, and it took advantage of its economic strength and highly efficient munitions factory to become involved in defeating the Nazis. American industry did not suffer any damage, its currency became the world's reserve currency, and it provided the largest proportion of foreign aid. In addition, the USA controls global oil resources through its vassal states. On the other hand, most parts of Europe and Asia were reduced to war-ravaged ruins.

Seen from Fig. 1, there was not a large population in North America in 1950, while it shared 1/3 of the global GDP. Numerous developing Asian countries, including the most populous China and India, added up to a mere 10% of the world's total. If we skip over 100 years rapidly to arrive at 2050, when nobody knows what will really happen, but we can consider the prediction of one of the world's largest banks, Citibank, as a starting point (see Fig. 2). The forecast for 2050 turns the world of 1950 upside down. Developing Asian countries will own half of the world's total revenue, while what North America owns will drop to a little more than 10 percent, with Western Europe having an even smaller share. The total output value of the former leading regions is predicted to be less than half of that generated by these former colonial and vassal states.

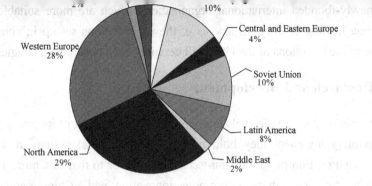

Fig. 1 The ratio of regional economic output to the world's total output value in 1950

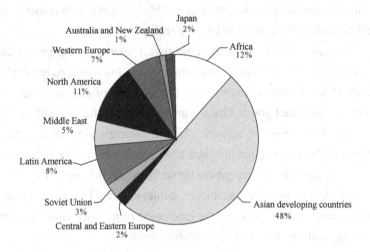

Fig. 2 Citibank's forecast for the proportional share of economic output of various regions all over the world to world GDP in 2050

The dominant position of the economy of Asian countries would have numerous consequences, with the political center moving from the USA and Europe to Asia. This would influence the existing composition of the United Nations, the Organization for Economic Cooperation and Development, the International Monetary Fund, and the World Bank, if they are still newly-founded international organizations which are more suitable to the new leading country. In any case, the organizations set up in compliance with the intentions of the USA will certainly have become meaningless.

Research and Development

Some Western intellectuals are opposed to this forecast of its future, and the primary argument they hold is that the educational system in the USA (including Europe in a certain sense) is superior to that of China. To begin with, American education promotes innovation, while Chinese education is based on authoritarianism, putting emphasis on spoon-feeding, which does not favor innovation or technological development in the long run. The quality of education in the Western world will make it impossible for the prediction of China's rising to become reality.

Please allow me to raise my objection. China is no longer the country that uses a cheap labor force and manufactures low-cost products. China is rapidly changing into a country with a huge army of engineers, technicians and highly educated youth. Great numbers of scientific research centers are emerging. In a series of sectors, Chinese enterprises are taking big steps forward in the value-added products chain, the combination of low cost and high technology has brought about powerful competitiveness. In a few years to come, China will be capable of achieving rapid growth through the improvement of efficiency and the innovation of products instead of gaining a leading position in the field of scientific research.

China's spending on scientific research is increasing, accounting for 1% of the GDP in 2004, which doubled in 2010 to reach 2%. As planned, it should attain 3% in 10 years. Meanwhile, an increasing number of foreign-capital enterprises are relocating their resources for scientific research to China.

Although the starting point is not high, the number of China's patent applications is on a sharp increase. Currently, China ranks No. 4, getting closer to the countries in front. Just from 2006 to 2010, international patent terms of quality, and actually fewer applications were approved, but people are ambitious about it, planning to rank in the world's top 5, which would actually take less time. A few enterprises have taken the lead — Huawei (in cooperation with Matsushita in Japan) has become a company with the largest number of registered patents over recent years.

China is even advancing at high speed in higher education. Presently China has 7 million university graduates, with the engineers and scientific & technological workers it cultivates outnumbering their counterparts in the USA, approximately 2 million to 400,000. In the next ten years, it is estimated that the number of students in colleges and universities will double. In fact, China's graduates majoring in science and engineering is increasing as well, 28,000 per year in comparison to 25,000 in the USA. It seems that the gap will widen. In spite of the fact that Chinese students have mixed abilities, many of them study diligently under the influence of Confucianism. On average, their mathematics and technical capability is superior to the level of their counterparts in the West.

Statistics show that Chinese researchers are reducing the gap with the West. The British Academy announced the rankings of published research papers of countries in the spring of 2011. The USA still ranked first, accounting for 20% of the amount of published literature, but the United States' share has declined rapidly over the past decade. China is on a sharp rise, currently taking up 11% of the amount of published scientific literature, more in chemistry and physics. China took merely a few years to leap from No. 4 place to No. 2. In the field of natural sciences and technology, China has already surpassed the USA. The United States still maintains its leading position in terms of the amount of published articles in the highest-profile journals, but the gap between the two countries is narrowing.

Underestimated Chinese Education

Various statistics show that the gap between China's ability to innovate and that of Western countries is narrowing. In a few decades, China will have although the opening trend of research work may experience ups and downs, it is moving forward. It seems overly confident to claim that Western education is so superior that China's demographic advantage might be offset.

There are about 100,000 Chinese students studying in US universities, and they are usually the top students of the year. Many of them stay in the USA after completing their studies, but the number of returnees is growing. Chinese authorities and university principals are trying to lure more top students to return home with generous salaries and research funding.

They may succeed. In the fall of 2010, the US magazine Newsweek said in an article that young hardworking Chinese people want to be educated in the top US universities, but are reluctant to work there. Upon graduation they are willing to return to work in China, since it is more vibrant, with a greater possibility of making money and getting promoted. When they retire, they prefer to settle down neither in China nor the USA, but in Europe — this is one place in the world with high-quality food and culture, and that is comfortable and quiet, just like a museum.

I sometimes wonder if China's education has some advantages which Western debaters have not acknowledged. But the International Student Assessment Report released by the OECD in 2010 compared and ranked the abilities of high school students in some countries, and reached the conclusion that students in Shanghai topped the list in reading and math, followed by those in South Korea, Hong Kong and Singapore, which are all countries or areas affected by the Chinese tradition of hard work. Students in the USA and Europe lag behind.

China's key universities are showing the ability to create patterns and incubators that nurture young entrepreneurs. In these areas, China has ambitious plans. In the next decade, over a hundred of the world's leading universities will be established, with two leaders entering the world's top 10. To support those promising entrepreneurs, some of the leading universities have set up science parks and innovative centers.

Creativity and education are often fiercely debated. Western ideas are challenged. In the winter of 2011, a paper on Children's education was published, and the author is a Chinese woman living in the United States — Amy Chua, a well-known law professor at Yale University. She had praised the Chinese woman as being a tigress in a book. She has also published the article "Why Chinese Mothers Are Superior?" in *Wall Street Journal*. This provocative article soon became the most commented one in the history of this newspaper.

Based on Confucianism, she claimed that the education of western children is permissive and hedonistic. We give children too many rights, and we give them all these rights too early, so that they just watch TV and play computer games, and they do not study hard, they do not do their homework, nor do they spend any time learning languages and appreciating classical music or literature. Chinese families have a different story. Parents pose requirements on their children, especially strict requirements concerning their schoolwork, and they require them to do their homework on time, in order to achieve better results.

Amy Chua said, Chinese parents think that what is best for children is not to give them abundant freedom or satisfy their needs immediately and easily, but on the contrary to exert strict requirements on them, counseling them, helping them prepare for the tough competition that is waiting for them in the future.

Most political comments in the USA showed their astonishment at her anti-humanism, but Chinese students outdo their Western classmates in natural sciences and mathematics. When tens of thousands of intelligent Chinese students graduate and embark on their careers as engineers, it should then astound us if their strict education is not reflected in their technical skills and in the increasingly sophisticated new products and services they provide. It is the same in the fields of Internet network building, infrastructural construction and green energy.

Creativity and an open-minded environment are considerably important, knowledge, and the brain perceives the connection, creativity will be promoted. Repeated training, lots of reading, and juvenile discipline can guarantee the acquirement of basic knowledge. The discipline of learning and the acquisition of basic skills and knowledge are the prerequisites for creativity and research, but the reverse is not true. The vast majority of people who we call genius have a solid foundation of basic skills and knowledge as well as long-term arduous research in their fields.

From my perspective, China's higher education will become increasingly open, and Chinese universities which make the utmost efforts to develop will recruit teachers, educators and other creative talents from every corner of the world. The challenges that China brings to the fields of scientific research and higher education should be taken seriously.

When China Rules the World

In the World Economic Forum in 2011 at the Davos Summit, I joined a discussion with several economic historians, of which the topic was how to view the development of the 21st century from a historical perspective, and what the biggest feature of this century is.

The unanimous view was great fusion. The main feature of the 19th and the 20th century was industrialization, the rise of Western countries, with Europe coming first followed by the USA. Third-world countries remained impoverished. This is a big difference, and the gap between the rich and the poor is seriously widening. But now history is beginning to turn to a new page, of which the leading change is the revenge of the poor countries. Their economies are starting to grow and are catching up. In this on-going race, those who are taking the lead are some big countries including China.

If China becomes a leading country, many fields would be influenced, and many areas would be branded. China usually emphasizes its own characteristics, in an aim to construct a country of "Chinese characteristics". The impact that China's economy will exert on the future world is self-evident, since China is destined to become the world's biggest super of such a huge population. I would like to remind you that I have predicted that China's economy will need only dozens of years to become several times as large as the total sum of the US and European economies.

At the same time, some Western countries will receive a hard blow by the debt crisis. The amount of US government bonds is so large that it is on the dangerous verge of hindering economic growth. Other countries like Italy and Japan have gone beyond the boundary. Some Western countries have to absorb the debt through inflation, or to renegotiate. Whatever they do, their freedom of movement and their ability to take action will be significantly restrained.

Economic power will bring political influence and in addition, it will generate the necessary resources to enhance their soft power — their cultural influence. When Chinese enterprises acquire foreign companies, Chinese management culture will be exported as well. When China uses a fraction of its foreign exchange reserves to radiate international influence of its state-owned television channels, its cultural values and culture will be disseminated. When China becomes the world's economic center, a growing number of economists and political experts will theorize a "Chinese miracle" and tell people how to learn from China.

Let me return to the 1950s, when I was born and Americans had the precedence. In the second half of the last century, the dominant role of Americans was only reflected in industrial production, trade and investment. American trademarks, food and culture swept the world. Think about hamburgers, jeans and Coca-Cola, as well as Hollywood, movie stars and rock music. What American tourists brought were not only dollars, but also glory. John F. Kennedy became the idol of many people throughout the world. We all learned much about American history, from the Civil War to the Kennedy assassination and 9•11, and we even seriously followed every US presidential election.

100 years later, probably around 2050, China may take over the role of the United States. At that time China's culture and politics may have more influence on us than what we can imagine today. Chinese food, including

conquer the world as well as Chinese style and Chinese design. We may watch Chinese TV in our own languages or even in Chinese. By then many of us will certainly have learned Chinese. A Chinese-style John F. Kennedy will probably fascinate us. When we are sick, we will use more herbs and acupuncture. We will admire Chinese sports stars. Hordes of Chinese tourists will cram into our famous historic and cultural sites.

It is not even because China as a superpower will have established more than a hundred Confucius Institutes in the neighborhoods, there will be other reasons why so many people study Confucius. The years 1949 and 211 B.C. will be as important as the year of 1632 and 1789 in our history books. We will take a closer look at the development of China's internal affairs, no matter whether it goes democratic or remains a one-party system.

Conclusion

The rise of China sparks strong emotions both in support of it and in opposition to it. It is not crystal-clear whether it is heaven or hell judging from the prediction. People may refute any judgment made on China, or disprove any prediction.

China is a one-party nation, but its citizens enjoy unprecedented freedom.

China is a poor country, but its middle class and its powerful wealthy upper class that is rolling in money are expanding.

China poses a threat to the environment and to the climate, but its investment in green technology overtakes that of all other countries.

China takes jobs from traditional industrial countries, but our standard of living has improved by lowering the prices of consumer goods.

China is expanding and has created a new balance — it has restored the balance broken by Western countries and the imperialist countries when China was going through a debilitating period.

China is colonizing Africa, without using force and slavery as Europeans have done, but by means of providing them with money and export markets instead.

leading country. If it does not spark any emotion, it is abnormal. It is what has always happened when a powerful new country came onto the stage to challenge the existing powers in history. We Europeans are well aware that, because over the past century a rising great power used force and blood to change the original power structure, Europe was twice reduced to a place where a world war broke out.

China's rise is quite distinct from the situation in which Germany, Japan and the USA challenged the Soviet Union respectively. China is much larger than they are. China has a much longer history, and has a different self-concept — it does not deem itself a competitive nationalist State, but a better ancient civilization bearing a civilized mission. China thus requires a greater international State than the previous superpowers did. The rise and breakthrough of it would have enormous political, economic and cultural impacts.

In the west, people think that the primary concern of Chinese leaders regards the issues related to us, such as the RMB exchange rate, trade agreements and international diplomacy, but nothing is further from the truth. China is so large, and it has so many domestic problems, that its leaders have to be swept off their feet to deal with domestic problems.

These problems are considerably tough to tackle. Chinese leaders have to transform impoverished rural areas with leftover traces of the planned economy into modernized and urbanized market economies covered by social insurance. They have to transform the State's energy supply system and infrastructural construction, so as to make the State's economy greener. They have to promote an enormous investment as well as the most important urbanization project in human history. They are also supposed to tackle the problem of population aging and opposition from the youth; moreover, they have to start setting up a social insurance system from scratch. Additionally, they have to withstand all kinds of tensions and maintain the unity of the State at the same time. All of these aspects have to be completed in the time-span of two generations, and what this country has is the largest population, the oldest State machinery, and the most ancient civilization.

In addition, they also want to retain the power of the Communist Party, predict whether they will succeed in remaining a one-party State or whether they will be forced to reform to another system. Nowadays, the Communist Party's goal is to preserve the one-party system through reforms. There are several possibilities. The Communist Party can buy popularity through the expansion of intra-party democracy, and develop a one-party State which will be more open to public opinions through individual voting.

If reforms are not achieved, society will become more rigid, and the one-party dictatorship will be oppressive, resulting in hostile conflict that would be difficult to resolve. One side is the party State, while the other side includes the economic sector and the public and international society. But the situation is quite clear, Western multi-party parliamentary democracy is not on the current agenda. On the other hand, people should not underestimate the Communist Party's ability to respond to new challenges. Although the Communist Party is a Leninist cadre party, it has also learned modern management and the techniques that win over public support.

The best result would of course be that China is able to successfully improve its standard of living, build a more harmonious and greener country, listen to public opinions, and continue to move towards democracy step by step. In this way, the entire human race will take a major step forward.

Therefore, we wish China success, and we will also make efforts to build a more open and more democratic country.

4

What Kind of Economic Reform Does China Need

Li Daokui

Li Daokui
Mansfield Freeman Professor of Economics at School of Economics and Management, Tsinghua University, Doctoral Supervisor and Distinguished Professor of the "Cheung Kong Scholars Program," Former member of the Monetary Policy Committee of the People's Bank of China and member of the 11th National Committee of the CPPCC, Dean of the Department of Finance, Tsinghua University, and Director of the Center for China in the World Economy (CCWE).

The deteriorating international environment, increasingly obvious social conflicts, and challenging economic structure adjustment…all these problems await the new reform of the economic system. Indeed, the numerous problems of China must be solved through a new reform of the economic system at a much deeper level. Therefore, it also requires that academics make new breakthroughs in their critical thinking on these critical issues. What was lost during this monotonous repetition of the catchwords used in the past decade-plus is the stature required of academics, and what has emerged from such repetition is the resistance in so many different ways by all sections of society.

Three Defects in the Present Discussions About Reform

The present discussions about reform, despite the great number and wide coverage, mostly share some conspicuous defects.

First, many discussions are only kept at the level of the vision of development and reform, and such visions tend to be confined to oversimplified catchwords, such as: to construct a socialist market economy with Chinese characteristics; to construct a good market economy and avoid a bad market economy; to construct the market economy based on laws; to construct the market economy with clearly-established ownership; to construct the market economy with sustainable development and giving consideration to fairness and efficiency…These wordings are undoubtedly correct and even beautiful, but if the discussions about reform are only kept at this level, it is impossible to provide theoretical guidance to the reform that is presently stagnant in many areas.

Second, many discussions about specific reform measures are not properly oriented. For example, as to the reform of individual income tax, many discussions are confined to the taxable threshold, neglecting many more important aspects: such as, what is the purpose for an individual income tax? Does the secondary allocation within the economic system of China primarily rely on the system of individual income tax or the institutional arrangements of other areas? Or, we may even ask: to what extent does China's economy need the secondary allocation? Discussions about property tax are confined to whether the increment or the inventory should be taxed, and whether the first property or the second property should be taxed. These discussions are obviously very technical, but some more basic issues are being neglected here. For example, what is the purpose of a real estate tax? What is the proper long-term policy for the real estate industry? And there are some greater issues, such as: what is the basis for the revenue of public finance in China; does it come from the production materials that have been long held by the state, or from the taxes collected from the links of production and circulation or wealth inventory? How much should China's government spending be? With regard to private enterprises, most discussions are focused on how to boost their development, but the more important concern should be: what is the best forms of ownership in China's future economic areas, the German model in which family businesses jointly control enterprises with the government, the Japanese model of socialized shareholding, or the American model in which majority shareholders control production materials in collaborating with the financial market?

Third, what we have learned from the comparative studies of different market economic systems in the contemporary era is not enough. To a great extent, we are consciously focused too much on the American-style market economic system. Undoubtedly, as the biggest economy in the world, the US has some attractive aspects in their economic system, but it is undeniable that the US has its remarkable uniqueness, hence the so-called "American exceptionalism." Of course, there are other rather different but very developed modern market economic systems in the world, such as the German, the Japanese, the Singaporean, which serve as important references for us to go for the next round of reform of our market economy and we must study and learn in a comprehensive way.

To Reform the Way of Reform in an Era of Limited Authority

The three problems with the discussions about reform as stated above are probably not the most important. The most important is that the way of discussing reform needs to be reformed, because we have entered an era of limited authority. In an era of limited authority, the official power of government and its decision-makers will not necessarily be lessened, but the power of decision-making and execution is clearly limited. One of the main reasons is that the public air their opinions via the internet and other media, forming an increasingly stronger pressure of public opinions; and another reason is the diversification of the interests within the existing system causes the process of government's decision-making to be influenced by the canvassing of various stakeholders and the process of execution to be constrained in various ways. In an era of limited authority, the academic authority is also limited. If it seems that scholars remain influential in terms of some issue or topic, it is generally because their views are just an echo of the popular thinking and public opinions, rather than a reversed mechanism.

For the present, most discussions about reform basically start and end with "how the reform should be carried out." It is potentially assumed that the discussants of reform are the designers and executors of the reform. Therefore, in most cases, the discussants raise proposals on reform based on their understanding of the target systems for society and economy of China, and such understanding of the target system for China's future market economy is normally based on individual preference. The analyzers who prefer and respect individual freedom and individual will are more willing to stress that the target reform should be the market-dominant economic system; on the contrary, the discussants are in favor of social fairness and order rather than individual freedom and will and therefore stress that China's future economic system should be the market system with government interference. The problem lies that, in many discussions, the individual preference of participants is hidden and the focus of debates is on the conclusion. The conclusion is not fit for debate if it is assumed differently.

Why is it necessary to break through these conventional practices with which the individual understanding of the goal of future market economic reform is defined as the direction for China's future reform? The reason is very simple: the basic social and political structure of China has been shifted from a reform designer with considerable authority or even absolute authority to a reformer with limited authority. There emerges the reality that neither party, including the government, is authoritative in today's Chinese society. None of academics, government sectors and government's top decision-makers has the same authority as in previous reforms.

On the other hand, the interest concerns in China's society are very much diversified. Three decades ago, the social hierarchy, composed of workers, peasants, civil servants and intellectuals, was simpler, while such simple division is no longer applicable. Today, the people who create public opinions and influence decision-making include business owners, stock investors, property owners, houseless groups, urban migrant workers, and even some foreigners. In such a diversified society, for the purpose of reform, the decision-makers without absolute authority must create a common understanding among the public and obtain the understanding and support of the majority, rather than being able to enforce any reform.

How to create a common understanding among the public and how to boost the meaningful reform of a socialist market economy? This question has been transformed to how to identify the preferences of the majority of society. That is to say, how to identify the conditions that constrain the advance of social reform. Put in another way, the way of discussing reform today should be transformed from "how should the reform be carried out according to me" to "what kind of reform shall the majority of society need, what are the basic preferences of society and the constraints, and based on these basic preferences and constraints, if we carry out the reform in the forms of A, B, and C and the results in the future would be X, Y, and Z, then whether these X, Y, and Z results in the future would commensurate with the basic preferences of society?" In other words, the academics' role is changing, from prescribing solutions to cure the society, to providing a menu to the society, along with some advice through rational analysis; that is, telling the social public and decision-makers what are the options for the reform, what will the result of each option in the future be, and whether these results would be better or worse than what they are today as judged by the public's taste.

I think this should be the basic model in which the academics discuss about the direction of China's future reform.

The Social Endowment of Economic System: The Basic Variables Determining the Economic System Reform

Based on the above way of thinking, it is necessary for us to discuss reform based on the basic preferences of society and basic constraints, so it is fair to call it the social endowment of China's reform, just like the endowment of nature. What is this endowment comprised of? There are three broad variables.

The first variable is the public's rationality about the market economy, that is, what the public understands about the market economy and how they are capable of operating in the market economy. The operation capability of the public in a volatile capital market is completely different across areas. For example, the public of Hong Kong is obviously more rational than the public of the Mainland, because they know better how to respond to a volatile stock market and real estate market. Even in Mainland China, people show different degrees of rationality about the market in different areas: the public of the coastal areas, like Jiangsu, Zhejiang and Fujian, feature stronger market rationality than those in the inland areas. Of course, it is evolving, for knowledge spread and the public keep learning.

The second variable is the public's preference between social order and individual freedom. With regard to this, Andrei Shleifer, an economist at Harvard University, particularly stresses in his famous articles of "The New Comparative Economics" that the choice made between social order and individual freedom varies in different communities. It is generally believed that the American society stresses individual freedom, while the countries on the European Continent, like Germany, are more likely to stress social order. Then what about the Chinese society? We are justified to believe that, compared to the US and western countries, the public of China tend to prefer order. Of course, "social order" used here should be understood in a broad sense. It not only includes a low crime rate, but also income gaps and differences in welfare, as well as the loss of welfare caused by various economic fluctuations. As to this issue, it is also fair to believe that the public in different areas in China have difference preferences.

A third endowment-like variable determining the social and economic system is the government's capability, i.e. whether the government is capable of efficiently implementing a set of economic systems and policies. This is obviously a critical variable. Governments of some countries or some regions are more capable, such as the Singaporean government, which is able to realize a low corruption rate and high efficiency in implementing a set of economic systems; on the contrary, governments of some developing countries are prone to corruptions, low capabilities and inefficient implementations. For China today, it is unsafe to call it an unalterable variable. With the advance of the reform of the political system and the government's higher accountability to the public, this variable will also change. In addition, the government's capabilities vary in different areas.

Three Dimensions of Modern Market Economic System

The modern market economy is very complex. How shall we provide an incisive summary of the differences between the systems of a modern market economy? Based on the overview of the existing literature, I believe three basic dimensions may be concluded.

The first dimension is the basic institutional arrangement of production and exchange.

The institutional arrangement of production organization is perhaps comparatively more important. There are different institutional arrangements, including the Japanese model of highly socialized controlled ownership, the American model in which majority shareholders manipulate the economy through the capital market, and the European model in which family business control is combined with government interference, which may differ from each other a great deal. It is particularly interesting to note that the institutional arrangement of production organization, which tends to be narrowly understood as a property ownership arrangement, is generally built-in and derived from the institutional arrangements of other relevant systems. Here are some examples. The inheritance tax in Japan is extremely high and it is hard for the family to hold the enterprise. In Germany, the capital operation is often limited, so the family is able to control the family business longer and in a more stable condition.

The institutional arrangement of transaction may also vary greatly in different economies. An extreme situation is the system of a planned economy, including note-based supply and distribution per capita. The other extreme is the institutional arrangement of a free transaction market which is absolutely determined by price. There are consecutive and infinite choices between these two extremes. Purchase restrictions or price restrictions are closer to the institutional arrangement of a planned economy. Another example is that, generally, the auto market is taken as the market for completely free transactions, but it is not true. Just imagine. If a consumer wants to buy a car of a somewhat unique model, like the Mercedes-Benz luxury sedan with a manual shift gear, from overseas, such a transaction may not always be realized as the consumer wishes, because the government has various standards on environmental protection and safety of auto products, while it is necessary to go through a complicated approval procedure to import a sedan of a certain model.

The second basic dimension is the institutional arrangement maintaining the stable operation of a market economy.

It is undeniable that a modern economy has the basic built-in volatility and such volatility is huge. The financial crisis provides this evidence. In order to cope with the built-in volatility, modern economies must be facilitated with a set of basic institutional arrangements.

First, it is the assortment and provision of public goods. It is essential to define what kind of products and services are public goods, which are hence to be provided by the state. Different economies have different understandings with this regard. For example, so far, the UK and Japan obviously think some basic journalistic and media services are public goods. Therefore, the BBC and NHK are both invested by the State and supervised by the government; the US does not have such a tradition. Here is another example. Basic housing service is taken as being the nature of public goods, so it is directly provided by the government, while it is taken as being private goods in the US in most cases.

Should we carry out income redistribution? Should we narrow the income gap through income redistribution in order to create a basic harmony in society? This issue is understood differently across societies, so the relevant institutional arrangements vary tremendously. The welfare system is a basic institutional arrangement to support the stable operation of the economy. It was first initiated by the UK and energetically promoted in Germany in the last century. The establishment of a basic welfare system is critical to supporting a stable economy.

Public finance is a fundamental system maintaining the stable operation of an economy, and it also involves many specific institutional arrangements. Some of the concerns could be: Is the income basis for public finance provided by state-owned enterprises or tax income? Should the state control a part of profitable assets and some non-productive financial assets?

The management systems of the macro economy, such as the management of the Central Bank, CSRC and CBRC, are also critical to a modern market economy. Even the most conservative libertarians would accept this point. Milton Friedman stressed repeatedly that, before the breakout of a financial crisis, the central bank must print a large number of banknotes, which is its natural duty; in addition, the central bank needs to be coordinated with the Ministry of Finance, instead of dealing with it single-handedly. Moreover, the institutional arrangement supporting the operation of an economy is market regulation, which involves some important issues, such as whether it is necessary to supervise relevant financial institutions to a great extent and whether it is necessary to carry out ongoing monitoring of their quantity of capital and degree of risk, or even to collect punitive taxes, and so on.

The third basic dimension is the mechanisms of settling conflicts of interest and allocation of rights.

It is inevitable for the interest groups in an economy to have conflicts of interest with each other, while it is impossible for these conflicts to be completely settled through the price mechanism of the market and friendly negotiation. Ronald Coase also believes that it is necessary to set a binding court as the background in order to maintain market operations. Allocation of rights is closely related to this. Who owns what rights determines how the parties to transactions carry out their negotiations, as is repeatedly stressed by Coase. In fact, the key point of the Coase theorem is to highlight the importance of allocation of rights. That is to say, it is only when rights are clearly divided and meanwhile there is a just third-party contractual executor that it is possible for both parties to a market transaction to carry out efficient negotiations and achieve the results of Pareto Optimality.

Special stress needs to be put on the role of the legal system in terms of this. There is a tendency that the legal system is defied in China, where the legal system is believed to be omnipotent. This is worth careful study. The legal system itself cannot be operated in a vacuum. In reality, two groups are superior in a legal system. One is the strong group or the wealth class in the market, who tend to be superior in the operations of the legal system, because they are able to engage the most excellent lawyers and utilize relevant resources to win a case. The other is the government, who tends to be the stronger side in a legal system, and it is difficult for a commoner to win a case in which the government is indicted. Therefore, the normal operation of the legal system must be supported by a set of relevant mechanisms, in particular, certain supervision measures. For example, the government's supervision may constrain the high wealth class's strong power over the legal system. Meanwhile it is also necessary to constrain the government's natural advantages in the legal system in some open ways, such as through public media, and in the way of division of power in the government.

Another important concern about the legal system is who shall make the laws. Different countries have their own ways of dealing with this. Under the British and American systems, the law-making power is delegated to courts and judges to a great extent; on the European continent, however, the law-making power is executed by relevant government sectors on behalf of the state. In

China presently, it is basically for the government to dominate the law-making. We have seen a lot of defects in this type of government-dominated law-making.

What Type of Economic Reform Does China Need

In discussing this issue, we must make it clear what is the social endowment of China's economic system. In terms of the rationality about the market economy, China's social endowment is still evolving. On average, the public of China are not as rational as the public of developed countries which have been experiencing a market economy for a long time. In terms of preferences to social order or individual freedom, the public of China, owing to the education of the feudal traditions and Confucian culture for thousands of years, are more preferable to social order than the public of, for example, the US. At the same time, the execution capability of the local governments of China varies greatly across regions and areas. For example, the execution capability is stronger and there are fewer corruptions in the area of the college-entrance examination, and the situations of other areas are far from this situation.

Given these social endowments, what kind of economic system reform does China need? First, the vision should be broadened from the American modern market system to the economic systems of the developed countries on the European Continent (Germany and Holland in particular) and in Asia (Japan, South Korea and Singapore). In some key areas, including the arrangements of ownership and control power of big enterprises, housing, commercial banks, basic welfare policies and education and training, systematic analysis, study and imitation should be carried out. Compared to the US, the endowment in economic systems of these countries are more similar to China, hence worth serious study.

Second, a somewhat indisputable conclusion is that China's reform should start with substantial delegation of power. Local governments are supposed to carry out their reform projects based on their situations and characteristics. Owing to great differences between the social endowments in the economic systems of different areas, local governments should take great initiatives to seek the direction of reform that is applicable to their areas. For example, as to the issue of land ownership, the rural residents of Zhejiang and Jiangsu feature higher market rationality than those in the central and western areas, so it is good for the former to take the first step.

One simple deduction is that the reform carried out by relying upon law-making may not necessarily best apply to the reality. China is a large country and there are large differences between social and economic endowments in different areas. If the reform is carried out uniformly by relying upon law-making, the results may not necessarily be favorable, even if the laws that have been made may be enforced.

Third, China's reform of the economic system should be adaptable enough. The reform cannot succeed in a day. The social endowment of the Chinese public is continuously evolving, the market rationality is increasingly improving, the preference to social order or individual freedom is always changing, and the government's execution capability is also changing — the reform itself is essentially driving the government to improve its execution. Therefore, it is flexibility, rather than rigidity, that is to be emphasized in the reform of China.

Therefore, a basic conclusion is that: the reform for the present stage should be carried out through broadening our vision and delegating powers, allowing local governments to seek the direction of reform of their areas based on their realities, and the reform will be carried out in the way of delegating powers and always evolving, instead of the top-down and uniformed way. This is also helpful for enterprises to have a bigger room for choice between different areas, and the choices of enterprises will help to improve the initiative and efficiency of reform of the areas.

5

China's Economic Growth Gradually

Slows Down

Wei Sen

Wei Sen
Professor at Fudan University, director of the Research Institute for History and Economic Thought at Fudan University. His works mainly include "The Social Order of Economic Analysis: An Introduction", "Economics and Ethics", "Culture and Order", "Economics and Philosophy: The Philosophical Foundation of the System Analysis", "Economic Theory and the Market Order", "The Rule of Law and Democracy", and so on.

to China's economy benefiting from the "marketization dividend" and the "demographic dividend," in the situation that both dividends are almost "eaten up," China's future economic growth will mainly rely on eating "the dividend derived from the reform of the system and the construction of a democratic nomocracy."

Why do we think that China's economy is gradually slowing down?

The subject of today's roundtable discussion is "searching for a new economic growth point." I would like to introduce a basic thought: China's economy has roughly entered the middle and late term of industrialization — if not the end, which largely determines the fact that China's rapid economic growth is slowing down, and is gradually entering a period of medium-speed growth.

Prof. Lin Yifu again communicated his optimistic expectation for the next 20 years that China's economy has more than an 8% growth potential. Yifu came to this conclusion, as he has explained just now, on the basis of the level of the GDP per capita. Since China's current GDP per capita is over 5,000 dollars, Yifu judges that China's gap with the USA is roughly the same as the gap between the USA and Japan in the 1950s, Singapore in 1967, Korea and Taiwan region between 1975 and 1977; and these countries and regions all took advantage of their own "natural endowments" — in order to achieve a high-speed growth of 8% over a 20-year period. Based on these facts, he predicted that China potentially has an 8% GDP growth rate for the next 20 years.

I am less optimistic than Prof. Lin Yifu is. I feel that, in the next 20 years, if China's economy can maintain a steady average annual GDP growth of 5% to 7%, that would be great. Thus, it seems inappropriate for our future governmental decision-makers and people in all walks of life to "do impossible things," going against the inverse trend of economic development, trying to maintain a growth rate of 8%, making every effort to maintain an unsustainable economic growth rate.

My conclusion is based on the following two reasons:

To begin with, on the surface, the "Troika" of China's economic growth analysis of it, and I totally agree. Here I would like to add some views: after a rapid growth over more than two decades especially during the last 10 years after China's entry into the WTO, exports have more or less reached their peak, and in a few years to come, the contribution of net exports to the GDP will be considerably insignificant, or even negative; on the other hand, the golden era of China's investment has been fading away, and the growth in China's consumption has been restrained by many factors: a long-time and continuous decline in household income within the national income, and other factors, which will fail to support a rapid economic growth in China in the future, and will, on the surface, determine a gradual decline in China's economic growth in the coming years or even over a longer period of time. Besides, according to the modern economic history of the world, a period of rapid economic growth in any country has coincided with a period of rapidly increasing investments. When an economy, which has been stimulated by a large amount of investments in the GDP, becomes driven by a growth in consumption, it means that, with rare exceptions, this economy is going through a change from high-speed growth to mid-or-low-speed growth.

Why are we saying that the golden age of the growth of China's investment is over? To answer this, we might look at three factors that are restricting China's growth of investment: first, the peak period of real estate investment is over. According to the research report released by the People's Bank of China and the Southwest University of Finance on May 13, 2012, China's homeownership rate is as high as 89.68%, much higher than the world average of 60%, almost the highest in the world. This fact, in turn, actually explains why the period of rapid investment growth in real estate will naturally come to an end. When? Regarding a further increase in real estate investment by China's future urbanization, within China's current system, institutions and cultural tradition, we do not have a clear picture of how China's future urbanization will develop and evolve. As seen at least from the existing economic situation, the next cycle of real estate development is coming.

Second, China is faced with sluggish exports and overcapacity as well as profits of China's enterprises have generally been gradually declining, a lot of enterprises are suffering losses, are short on self-owned funds, and the enterprises, which are not involved in exports, also have a weakened driving power for expansion.

Third, and most important, since the beginning of the 21st century, the golden age when a round of massive investments in infrastructural construction was promoted at all levels of government, including highways, high-speed rails, airports, harbors, government buildings, and even most of the major cities' infrastructural construction, is nearly completed and saturated. Even if some new projects have been launched, it is impossible to be fully underway on a large scale like several years ago. Of course, according to the deployment of the national "Twelfth-Five" plan, there is a growth potential in infrastructural construction such as highways, railways, airports, subways and water conservancy work, but the debt rate of local governments is already so high, and coupled with a slow-down in the growth of the tax revenue due to the falling economic growth rate, it puts greater pressure on the expenditure of people's livelihood, much greater restraint on risks in local areas, and thereby the expansion of investments in the construction of infrastructures is restrained. Even according to a recent research conducted by the team led by Liu Shijin from the Center for Economic Research of the State Council, it is expected that the growth rate of fixed asset investments will be below 20%. Investment opportunities are reduced and investment is shrinking; in addition to the huge debt caused by previous investments, all of the above have determined that the growth rate of China's economy is gradually slowing down.

Furthermore, the idea that the Troika is underpowered has only pointed out some superficial elements of the short-term downside of the growth of China's economy. However, the more sophisticated problem is that, after the rapid growth of China's economy for over 30 years, especially after China's admittance to the WTO, foreign trade and exports have increased rapidly, people's living standard has risen (including the fast growth of household appliances, automobiles, etc.) and a relatively rapid urbanization, especially decades, so far, China's economy has basically come to the mid-to-late period of industrialization, if not the end. Therefore, at the current stage of China's economic development, the marginal rate of return on capital investments, in almost all of the sectors, is declining year by year, and in the real world this shows that business opportunities in every sector may be decreasing and diminishing.

China's overall marginal rate of return on capital has already declined. Here, I specially recommend an article that Prof. Wu Xiaoying published in *Caijing* (2012, Issue 27). According to his years of follow-up study, from 1955 to 1999, China's marginal rate of return on capital "declines at a surprising speed." Therefore, Wu Xiaoying draws the conclusion that "when an economy hits the bottom, the efforts of investment made to achieve growth are at the expense of efficiency." I overwhelmingly agree with this judgment. In fact, several research reports made by Dr. Peng Wenbo's research team here also reflect and support this idea.

The general decline in the marginal rate of return on capital means that the potential growth rate of China's overall economy is slowing down. I come to this conclusion on the theoretical grounds that I have benefited from some insights obtained early this year from re-reading Keynes' *Monetary Theory — Theory of Monetary Reform* (1926) and *The General Theory of Employment, Interest and Money* (namely *The General Theory*, 1936). In Chapter 30 of the *Monetary Theory*, Keynes emphasized and pointed out, "I would like to draw historians' special attention to the obvious conclusion that: during the period of various countries' profit expansion and contraction, it is unusually consistent with the period when China's economy boomed and slumped." Keynes felt it was not enough to point this out, and added: "This book's major viewpoint is that, a country's wealth is not enhanced from the expansion in revenue, but from the expansion in profits; that is to say, it happens when price surpasses the cost and skyrockets."

Keynes' judgment mentioned above is a remarkably great and profound theoretical discovery. The core idea of what he said is that a country's heyday and recession are closely related to the marginal rate of return on return on capital is a significant economic indicator of a country's economic prosperity and depression. Of course, experts on economy know that, in terms of the technology of macroeconomic analysis, the marginal rate of return on capital in all sectors has kept the downward trend for years, which is not the problem of destocking, but the problem of the trend of economic growth. To put it in an evocative way, when all sectors feel it impossible or hard to make money, it means that a country's economy has almost hit its peak in a certain historical period.

Based on this in-depth consideration, in my interview "The Great Transformation of the Chinese Economy" in May, and especially in another lengthy interview, "Take the Pulse of China's Economy," released on the FT website on August 10th this year, I talked about the same thing: China's economic growth is gradually declining, which appears to be irreversible and a natural trend.

Finally, I would like to point out that I initially felt the gradually downward trend of China's economic growth partly because for many years I have been studying the history of the literature of world economic history and China's economic history. Since 1979, China's economy has experienced over 30 years of continuous growth, with an average annual growth rate of more than 9%.

Despite the short-term fall of economic growth in 2009, we can say that we have experienced a 10-year golden period of growth, with an average annual GDP growth rate of more than 10%. Such a prolonged and rapid economic growth is unprecedented in human history.

Seen from the modern history of human beings and modern economic history, in the modern-day rise of Europe, industrialization has contributed to the take-off of a country's economy, with an initial stage of rapid growth, then medium-speed growth, and finally a long-term sluggish period. According to Prof. Angus Maddison's research during his lifetime, Britain's compound growth rate between 1830 and 1870 was 2.05%. In 1873, the first Great Depression ended. Then, from 1870 to 1913, it entered a period of medium-speed growth, with a compound growth rate of 1.9%. After 1813, unemployment rate of over 10% or even 20%. Until World War II came to an end, in around 1950, Britain stepped out of the British Disease with a wave of rapid global economic growth. Seen from the point of view of modern history, the rise of Germany's economy took around merely 30 to 40 years. Since Bismarck unified Germany after 1871, from 1871 to 1913, the average annual growth rate of Germany's GDP was 2.83%; then Germany was involved in World War I and its economy was reduced to ruins and depression. Japan is another example. Japan's postwar period of rapid growth lasted for 18 years, and it was in fact due to Japan's economic recovery from the ruins of the war that there was a wave of relatively rapid growth rates. From 1955 to 1973, Japan's GDP average growth rate was 8.89%, and the period between 1975 and 1990 was a period of medium growth, with a yearly average growth rate of 4.29%. After 1990, Japan entered a prolonged downturn. So far, the average annual growth rate over the past two decades is only 0.85% (See Fig. 1).

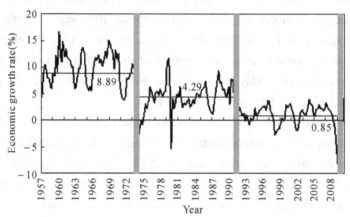

Fig. 1   1957–2009 Japan's economic growth trajectory

Having a thorough look at the modern and contemporary history of mankind in some countries, in contrast to the current stage of the development of the Chinese economy as a whole, I have a less mature judgment: at present, China's economy is roughly at the stage that Japan's economy experienced gradually shifting from rapid growth to medium-speed growth.

Based on this judgment, I made an appeal at the Guangzhou Lingnan Forum: it is not horrible for China to enter a period of medium-speed growth, but what is horrible is that we are not aware of that, and we artificially approve and urge some blind investment projects that governments have advocated — like the Zhanjiang iron and steel project "Kiss Growth," to artificially protect an 8 percent growth rate, and thus reverse the inevitable law and the inevitable trend of economic development. This is a waste of resources on something that is unachievable. In doing so, in a short term, local governments at all levels and statistics offices will fabricate fake statistics regarding economic growth, and even reluctantly cast some irrecoverable costs and fabricate some inefficient investment projects; and, in the medium to long term, this will throw the Chinese economy into a deep Depression!

Just now Prof. Lin Yifu said he still advocated relying on the government's investment in further infrastructure to sustain an 8% growth. I feel that the concept of this policy proposal deserves sympathy and understanding; as I have pointed out above, a period of rapid economic growth in any country is in fact a period when investments in fixed assets expand rapidly, but today we should be aware that this policy guidance probably has its limitations and potential risks.

I have made a rough calculation. During the 3 years from 2009 to 2011, the total social fixed asset investments in China added up to 80.49 trillion yuan, an annual average growth rate of 25.8%. If in 2012, the government loosens its monetary policy, and fiscal stimulus is strengthened, in these 4 years, the total social fixed asset investments in China will add up to more than 110 trillion yuan, twice the total GDP in 2012, surpassing China's broad money M2 and China's total bank deposits. Only when we understand such massive investment in fixed assets, can we truly understand why in the past 3 or 4 years when the recovery of the global economy was struggling through doldrums, China achieved an annual growth rate of over 9%, and then we can understand that the downside of China's economic growth will maintain a long-term sustainable growth promoted by such a sky-high sum of investments. In the general trend in which the marginal rate of return in the capital of the whole society is down (this downward trend, in return, is precisely an inevitable contributor to the rapid growth of this sky-high sum of investments), when the invested projects are not profitable, and most enterprises earn negative profits, who would repay the debt? Who will pay for an over 100 trillion yuan's investment in fixed assets? This is the appeal I have made again and again over the past few years according to the cycle of business theory by the Austrian School Mises and Hayek: be alert to the potential risks of China's economy. In accordance with the analysis of economists in this school, when the time to repay is due, and when the investment is liquidated, the Great Depression will not be far away.

Where is the new growth point in China's future economy?

Does being aware of the fact that China's economic growth rate will gradually slow down in the future mean that the government should completely withdraw or do nothing to intervene in future economic growth? Obviously not. Just now Yifu claimed in a keynote speech that in some time to come, we must continue to increase government investments in infrastructure, and regard the government as an important contributor to China's future economic growth rate.

I basically agree and support this point of view. In spite of the fact that over the past few years, the government has had a large number of improper investments and wasteful investments, and has left a huge debt burden on local governments at all levels; at the current stage of China's economic development, taking into account that all the levels of government actually take in 20 trillion yuan in revenue ("First Finance," land-transferring fees, various "extra incomes" and "income from out of system"), we should support the Chinese government to continue its investment in subways which can improve the people's livelihood and some public infrastructure in some regions and cities — especially in some Midwest cities. With respect to the financial system, I am in favor of the argument of scholars like Jia Kong that local governments should be given permission to issue bonds for

for building infrastructures will promote the local governments' bright financing, and more importantly, it will promote the market-based financing of the government of China, rather than rely on bank loans and on a variety of government financing platforms to conduct secret operations. Investment in infrastructure and financing through bank loans and government financing platforms has laid a huge risk on China's economy, and in fact has become an important channel and a hotbed for the rent-seeking and corruption of many officials. The investment of all levels of government in the construction of infrastructure by issuing bonds will reduce the burden on the banks, leaving the risk to the market, to investors themselves. It will also reduce the risk of the banking sector as a whole in the long run.

Although it is necessary to maintain a relatively high rate of investment especially the rate of investment in infrastructure, I personally think, from the perspective of national development strategies, in a gradual downward trend of China's economy, compared with the launching of larger-scale investments to maintain growth; we'd rather make efforts to look for a new point of growth when China gradually enters the period of a middle-income country and is about to enter a period of mid-speed growth.

Where is the new point of growth in China's economy? With respect to this question, in the recently published "New Structural Economics and Seek Prosperity," Prof. Lin Yifu proposed that in addition to relying on the government's investment in infrastructure, the new point of growth for China's future economy is supposed to be gained mainly relying on technological innovation and on the industrial upgrading of enterprises under the guidance and direction of the government. In fact, the Chinese government, especially NDRC, has done a lot in these areas over the past few years. Although it seems that there has been some success and some achievements have been made, there are many problems as well. For example, a large number of enterprises in the solar and polysilicon industry — like Wuxi Suntech and Jiangxi LDK — have become debt-laden and insolvent due to blind development, and these enterprises are some typical examples of enterprises that face the dilemma of collapse.

point of growth primarily lie for China's economy? I think that a contributor which has been mentioned frequently and that everyone talks about, but is actually overlooked in reality, is the development of the service sector, especially the financial service industry.

China's new economic point of growth perhaps may no longer count on a larger-scale launch of investments in fixed assets, but instead it should rely on the development of the service sector, particularly of the financial services sector — it does not seem to be a new theory, so therefore might not seem to be able to contribute to a new point of growth. I think the key to the problem is that we should understand this point from the basic theories of economics: the service sector, especially the financial services sector, does not provide services and financing for the manufacturing and real economy sectors, but the financial services sector itself also creates GDP.

Recalling the modern history of mankind, especially contemporary economic history, we find that economic development and social prosperity in all countries reflect not only the performance of scientific development and industrial upgrading in the manufacturing sector, but they also show that the market division is more refined, manufacturing becomes more circuitous, more transactions are made and the service sector emerges; as a result the proportion of the service sector in the GDP grows, especially the financial sector. In this context, the development of the service sector, or the national income created by the service sector takes up a larger share of the GDP, which is a typical example or an internal component of modern economic growth.

To illustrate this, we'd better ask ourselves this: In recent years, the total volume of China's material manufacturing sector has hit the top of the world, but so far China's GDP is just nearly half of the USA's GDP at present prices. What on earth is the reason? For example, according to the figures released by the International Steel Association in early 2012, China's crude steel production has reached 6.955 million tons (according to the figures released by China's Ministry of Industry and Information Technology in March 2012, China's steel output in 2011 was actually 730 million tons), amounting to 45.5% of the total global crude steel production 1.527 billion tons, more

India. In 2011, China's cement production was also up to 2.085 billion tons, taking up over 60% of the total global output. In 2011, China's coal output was 1.956 billion tons of oil equivalent, leaving the world's second-ranked America (556 million tons of oil equivalent) lagging behind, China's share of global production rising to about 50%. China produced 18.40 million autos in 2011, 4.7 million more than the 13.7 million produced in the USA.

In 2011, China's tonnage of completed shipbuilding was up to 68 million tons, which also ranked first in the world. In addition, according to the figures released on March 4, 2011 by the China National Bureau of Statistics, by 2010, China will have 220 kinds of production of industrial goods whose output will take up the largest share of global production in the world. Why is China's GDP not the largest in the world but only half that of the USA? The reason lies in the backward development of China's service sector — especially in the financial services industry; the share of value created by the service sector in the GDP is left far behind that of Western countries, and even smaller than that of India and some other developing countries (See Figs. 2 and 3).

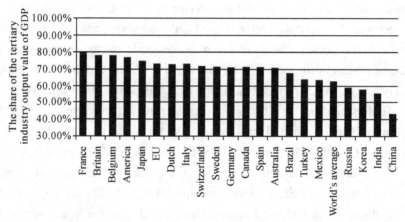

Fig. 2 The share of the output of the tertiary industry of some countries in the GDP for the year 2011

Source: wind, CICC data.

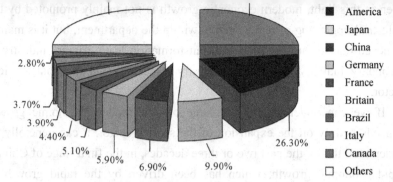

America
Japan
China
Germany
France
Britain
Brazil
Italy
Canada
Others

2.80%
3.70%
3.90%
4.40%
5.10%
5.90%
6.90%
9.90%
26.30%

Fig. 3   The share of the output of the tertiary industry of some countries in the output of the global tertiary industry for the year 2011
Source: wind, CICC data.

From Figs. 2 and 3, we can clearly see that although the output value of China's real economy sector far exceeded that of the United States, as for the development of the service sector and the tertiary industries, China is still far behind the United States and other developed countries, below the world average, even behind India (pro rata). For example, in 2011, the share of China's GDP created by the service sector in the total GDP is far smaller than that of the USA and some developed countries, which of the latter accounted for more than 70% on average. In 2011, in the United States within the 15.9 trillion dollars of the GDP, the value created by the service sector was more than 76% of the GDP. In the same year, in about 7.5 trillion US dollars of the GDP in China, the share created by the service sector took up only 43.1%, especially the financial services sector accounting for less than 7% (in Hong Kong, China, this index is 22%–25%, and Singapore 26%). This example fully shows that, the services sector, in particular the financial services sector which accounts for a large part, is the main component of modern economic growth.

Moreover, according to the statistics of CEIC DATA database, in 1950, the value of the US manufacturing sector took up 27.03% of the GDP, financial services accounting for only 11.49%. Sixty years later, in 2010, the proportion of the manufacturing output to the US GDP dropped to just

Seen in this light, modern economic growth is not mainly promoted by the industrial upgrading of real economy within the department, but it is mainly achieved due to the transition and transformation from primary industry to secondary industry and tertiary industry, especially the financial services sector.

If we can understand that a large part of modern economic growth depends mainly on the expansion of the service sector, it can generally be understood that in the past two or three decades, in the final stage of China's rapid economic growth, which has been driven by the rapid growth of China's real economy sector, the economic growth rate is on a downward trend, an appropriate national development strategy during the transformation phase of an economic society.

In the current pattern of China's economy and society, and in the current world economic environment, in order to maintain a stable and sustainable economic growth rate, it is not only inadequate but also dangerous to rely only on the government's investments in infrastructure. Entire dependence only on technological innovation and industrial upgrading, in light of the forefront of the current scientific and technological development of human society, can not constitute the main thrust for the future growth of China's economy. Now, in order to achieve a further enhancement of China's economy, China's economy has to maintain a relatively stable rate of growth. We have to follow the general rules of the modern social and economic development of mankind; but it seems that following the Western countries that have already walked the path of development of services, namely follows the road that Western countries have travelled in order to develop the service industry and financial services. Conversely, only when the financial market and financial services are flourishing can they be expected to provide services for the real economy sector, particularly technological innovation and the industrial upgrading of enterprises, and can they provide better services for investment and financing. More importantly, the development of the financial services industry and the booming of the stock market will in contrast enhance people's confidence in future investments look prosperous.

How to develop the service industry? In this respect, the economics profession and all sectors of the community have a large number of research reports and policy recommendations. I am here just to point out a seemingly empty but in fact essential problem: since the development of the service industry, especially the financial service industry, requires an environment of a well-ordered legal system, without further reform, especially in the political system, we cannot expect our service industry, especially our financial service industry, to make great progress. The reason is simple to say; if the modern democratic political system with the rule of law cannot be established, if the judiciary is always the hardest hit by corrupt government officials, and if the rent-seeking phenomenon by which government officials use the power they are invested with and the vast resources they control to conduct more and more, and more and more severe, corruption, then rule by law will exist in name only, resulting in the entire community experiencing increasing unfairness in social income and wealth ownership, as well as increasing social tension. If some private entrepreneurs feel insecure about the future and feel immensely uncertain, and thus transfer their assets abroad in succession, how will China be able to achieve a booming financial service industry and sustainable economic growth?

It is from this perspective that we think, if China's rapid economic growth over the past 30 years is mainly due to the dependence of China's economy on the "Marketization Dividend," and on the "demographic dividends" derived from the past as Prof. Cai Fang insists, under the circumstances that these two dividends are bound to be "eaten up," China's future economic growth will primarily count on eating "the dividends from institutional reform and building democracy and a legal system."

Two weeks ago, after I finished the report on China's current macroeconomic situation and its trend at the Guangzhou Lingnan Forum, a very specialized audience asked me this question: "Prof. Wei Sen, since China's overall marginal return rate on capital investment is declining, how can you expect China's stock market to boom?" This is a very good, very further scrutiny. Concerning this problem, you can ask two more questions one after the other, and you will find your answer:

(1) In the past three or four years, China's economy has remained at an annual GDP growth rate of over 9%, so why did China's stock market have the worst performance in the world, even worse than that of Greece and Spain?

(2) In past three or four years, the overall GDP annual growth rate of the United States was no more than 20%, but why did US Dow Jones and Nasdaq indexes keep touching new highs?

Once we get to the bottom of these two issues, we can easily foresee this scenario: China's stock market and financial market will keep shrinking, and China's financial service industry will not develop very much, mainly because of China's institutions. Therefore, we can come to the conclusion that without a fundamental reform of the system, China's financial service will not flourish, and China's stock market will not achieve real long-term and stable prosperity. This, on the other hand, shows that China's future economic growth will probably primarily count on the "institutional reform dividend." Perhaps it is because of this that all the Chinese people and even the whole world have so many expectations concerning the 18th National Congress of the CPC. We expect the new generation of Chinese governmental leaders to really make a difference, to deepen economic reforms, and meanwhile to steadily and progressively start political reform in China.

6

Direction of Economic System Reform

Wu Jinglian

Wu Jinglian
Senior Research Fellow for the Development Research Center of the State Council of the PRC, Member of the Standing Committee of the Chinese People's Political Consultative Conference and Deputy Director of the Economic Committee, Deputy Director of the Advisory Committee for State Information, and Deputy Director of the Academic Committee of the Development Research Center of the State Council, Chief Editor of the magazines of Reform, Comparative Studies and Journal of Legal and Economic Studies, Famous alumnus of Fudan University, and Doctor of Social Sciences in The Hong Kong Baptist University and The University of Hong Kong. Recipient of the Sun Yefang Award in Economics five times from 1984 to 1992. Honored with the International Academy of Management's (IAM) Award of Excellence in 2003, and the China Economics Prize – Outstanding Contribution to China's Economy Award in 2005.

The direction of economic systems reform is presently a common concern of many economists and even ordinary people of China. So far, for 30 years, China's economic reform has been carried out in the direction as defined during the Third Plenary Session of the 11th Central Committee of the CPC. But different opinions and choices emerged since the beginning of this century, so it seems that the reform has come to another crossroad, provoking a different choice. I am going to express some of my personal views below based on what I have been thinking about related to this issue.

More Focused on Top-Down Design and Overall Planning of Reform

The CPC pointed out two major points in formulating the "Twelfth Five-year Plan" in 2010. One is about the main line for the "Twelfth Five-year Plan," i.e. to realize the transformation of the economic development model; the other is about the overall reform, the drive to realize this transformation.

The "Outline of the Twelfth Five-year Plan" proposes that "it is imperative to push forward the reform in various areas with greater will and courage," and meanwhile requires us "to be more focused on the top-down design and overall planning of reform."

Since then, many sectors became engaged in exploring the "top-down design" for their own use, and academics also discussed what key areas to be chosen for reform and how to carry out the "top-down design" for the reform in these areas. "Top-down design" became a common topic for various central departments, such as finance and banking, and even for some specific reform projects, such as the reform of public hospitals. I think this is somewhat a misinterpretation of "top-down design."

What is "top-down design?" Why did it come about? These are the questions shared by many others.

Originally, "top-down design" is a term for Network Architecture. It means the design of a big system has to be started from top to down before the construction is initiated. When the Advisory Committee for State Information talked about the e-government network construction in 2001, they found that many local governments were interested in building their networks by purchasing the best computers and best peripheral equipment, rather than in the design of the whole system. For example, Academician Li Guojie, Head of the Institute of Computing Technology, China Academy of Sciences, proposed to "strengthen top-down design" through determining whether physical isolation or logic isolation should be set between the intranet and the extranet in government authorities. As pointed out by some IT scientists, for constructing an e-government network, a design at the top level, rather than from sub-systems, should first be in place. It is only in this way that it is possible for each sub-system to have inter-communication, compatibility and interaction. Mr. Liu He, then Deputy Director of the State Council Informatization Office and Director of the Advisory Committee for State Information, presided over this discussion.

Why Was It Proposed to Be "More Focused on Top-Down Design and Overall Planning of Reform"

Why was it proposed in the "Twelfth Five-year Plan" to "be more focused on top-down design and overall planning?" There could be two reasons. First, it is believed by many that a definite design for goal and program is always absent in China's reform, which is still "crossing the river by feeling the stones," without realizing that China did develop "top-down design" and overall planning for the "socialist market economy" in the last century and they need further improvement for the present stage. The other reason is that another "top-down design" occurred in the beginning of this century, so it is necessary for us to compare and find out which "top-down design" is more suitable to China's reality, more correct, and more realizable.

In my view, it is wrong to take our present stage as still being "crossing the river by feeling the stones." It was the way we tried in the early 1980s, because China had been isolated from the outside world for many years in terms of economic theories. A stereotyped opinion was that a socialist country must adopt the system of the Soviet Union, but when it was proved by many facts that this type of system did not work, the leaders were somewhat at a loss as to what type of system to adopt. Therefore, at that time, Chen Yun and Deng Xiaoping both pointed out that "we have to cross the river by feeling the stones now" and "let the stones guide us step by step." This situation had already changed by the middle of the 1980s.

In the middle of the 1980s, decision-makers, economists and the public all came to realize that the reform would not truly succeed only by "feeling the stones." So a proposal of "top-down design" was raised. But it was not called "top-down design", but rather "goal model."

Janos Kornai, head of the Research Department of the Institute of Economics, Hungarian Academy of Sciences, delivered an important speech on the goal model of reform at the "Bashan Cruise-Ship Conference" in 1985. He argued that the system models of a modern economy could be divided into the two categories of administrative coordination and market coordination, which were further divided into 4 sub-categories of direct administrative coordination, indirect administrative coordination, market coordination without macro control, and market coordination with macro control. Kornai was inclined to choose the market coordination with macro control as the goal of the reform. It was accepted by all. Later, the economic fluctuation in 1988 and the political volatility in 1989 led to divided opinions on what type of economic system China should build. After 1989, the belief in the planned economy became the dominating idea.

Deng Xiaoping proposed that "a socialist country may also practice the market economy" in December 1990 and February 1991. Since then, from the middle of 1991 to the middle of 1992, it took one whole year for the leaders of the CPC and the central government of China and the economists to seek this approach by combining theory and practice. Finally, it was at the 14th National Congress of the CPC in October 1992 that the goal of China's reform was established, i.e. a system of market economy in which the market plays a fundamental role in resource allocation. It is fair to say that this was the "top-down design" defined for China's economic reform. After this "top-down design" was defined, the "overall planning" of the economic reform was initiated, i.e. to study the reform programs for each area and how they worked with each other. Then, the Third Plenary Session of the 14th

Central Committee of the CPC held in November 1993 adopted the "Decisions on Several Issues Concerning Developing a Socialist Market Economy (50 Items)," formulating the overall planning of the market economy and detailed programs for each area. This Decision was proposed in great detail and was highly spoken of both home and abroad. From 1994, the reform was launched according to this overall planning. Then, the 15th National Congress of the CPC held in 1997 proposed to "adjust and improve the ownership structure," thus to initiate the "strategic structure adjustment" of the state-owned economy selectively, for the convenience of establishing the "pattern with the public sector remaining dominant and diverse sectors of the economy developing side by side." The continuously improved "top-down design and" overall planning of reform has been vigorously pushing forward the reform of the economic system of China and laying an institutional basis for the rise of China's economy.

But we have to realize that there is a big defect in the preliminary framework of the market economy that was established at the end of the 20th century. Such a defect is reflected in two aspects. One is that it still kept some key factors of the planned economic system, which were concentrated on the government's interference in the economic life and the state-owned economy's control of the market. The other is that the governance by law, that is essential to modern market economy, had not been set up.

Just because of this, the Third Plenary Session of the 16th Central Committee of the CPC held in 2003 adopted the "Decisions on Several Issues Concerning the Improvement of the Socialist Market Economy," calling for further reform in many important areas. But the reform had already come to the deepwater area, so the further the reform was pushed forward, the more and more power and interest of the local government and officials were to be affected, and there was a great obstacle to the reform. Owing to the advancement in reform which made China's economy begin to rise, government officials at all levels were complacent and did not think it necessary to further the reform. Under such circumstances, there was neither pressure nor drive, so the reform was beginning to slow down. The reform became stagnant, the market order was in chaos, and a worsened authoritative interference enlarged the institutional foundation for rent-seeking activities, so it became so increasingly corrupted that it was even harder for rigorous enforcement of laws to stop it. Meanwhile, the gap of wealth was continuously widened. In retrospect, the corruption that was represented by "official profiteering" that was earnestly criticized by the public in the end of the 1980s was no rival to the emerging corruptions in the new century.

Rampant corruptions and wider gaps of wealth provided chances for those supporting the old system and old line to employ the discourses of Populism and nationalism to misguide the public. It is true that, since the reform and opening up, the reform oriented in market, governance by law and democracy were constantly questioned and objected to by those supporting the old system and line. This kind of questioning voice, however, has become louder since the arrival of the new century, and has gained support from some vulnerable groups through wrong publicity. The so-called "prescription" or another "top-down design" proposed by them is to stop corruption and the widening gap of wealth by deploying the state machinery, and meanwhile to boost the dazzling achievements through immense investments through exerting the government's strong capability of mobilizing resources. As a result, a vicious cycle was created — the stronger the government's control was, the larger the institutional basis for rent-seeking became, and the worse the corruption was; when the corruption became more serious, it became more convincing to ask the government to strengthen the controlling force of government and state-owned enterprises (SOEs) under some wrong public opinion.

The initial form of the so-called "top-down design" is called "Beijing Consensus," which was later called the "China model." The main contents of it are to support the high-speed growth through immense investments by relying upon government and state-owned enterprises. This type of government-led developmental road was encouraged in the short-term policies of the governments of the West after the global financial crisis. It seemed that its "superiority" was supported by some short-term achievements. Some "show cases" emerged in the process, such as the "miracle of high-speed rail" hailed by the supporters of the "China model," the super-high-speed development realized in some places through local government's strong mobilization and input of huge resources, and so on.

So there became the dilemma of choosing between two different "top-down designs," i.e. the market economy based on governance by law and state capitalism. In my opinion, by proposing the issue of "top-down design" again, the "Twelfth Five-year Plan" is essentially defining a correct direction for future reform.

To Win a New "Consensus on Reform"

The changing situation of recent years shows the possibility of making a conclusion of the arguments over "top-down design" and forming a new "consensus on reform."

First, in recent years, more and more people, through analysis and discussion in terms of theory and historical experience, have realized that regression will take us nowhere. Second, the serious consequences caused by the model of "strong government and big state-owned enterprises" by economic development sectors and regions are recently becoming obvious. Therefore, there is a louder voice for pushing forward with the overall reform, both in the government and the public, and even the possibility of forming a new "consensus on reform."

This new consensus on reform is not completely different from the past, but goes further from the existing situation. For example, there are defects in the reform upsurge emerging after entering the 1990s, particularly after Deng Xiaoping's "speeches in the south." The most critical defect is that the political system reform was not mentioned together with the economic system reform as they were before 1992. In fact, the political reform was involved in the backward aspects in the process of reform in China, including the clear demarcation of government functions and the selective adjustment of state-owned enterprises. As Deng Xiaoping pointed out several times in 1986, if the political system was not reformed, it was impossible to succeed in the economic reform.

The "reform" in the "more focused on the top-down design and overall planning of reform" as proposed in the "Twelfth Five-year Plan" refers to "the reform in the areas of economy, politics, culture and society." So, our "top-down design" and overall planning should be the "top-down design" and overall planning of the overall reform rather than those of any single reform project.

Currently, there is an earnest discussion about the ongoing "top-down design" and overall planning of reform among people of all backgrounds. The discussion about the overall planning of economic reform largely covers three areas: the area of private goods, i.e. "the competitive area," including market opening, SOE structure adjustments, rural land reform, and financial reform; the area of public sectors, including financial and taxation reform, development of NGOs, and so on; and then the market regulation, including substantial review and approval, compliance regulation, anti-monopoly enforcement, etc.

The discussions about the political reform also largely cover three areas: governance by law, democracy and constitutional government. And further discussion is needed as to such issues as what these three areas embrace, whether they should be pushed forward in priority or synergistically.

"Top-Down Design" Needs to Be Combined with Grass-Root Innovation

As a colossal system, the social and economic system needs "top-down design" and overall planning in order to ensure the coordination and interaction between each sub-system. Nevertheless, it is important to listen to the demands of the public in the process of "top-down design", which is to be combined with the innovations from down to top and the inspiration and experience from the proactive exploration of local governments.

There are already some local reform experiments. Take Shanghai for instance. Years ago, the Shanghai municipal government began to require that state-owned capital be withdrawn from dozens of competitive industries and the government inspects how these policies are being carried out each year. The pilot project of the VAT expanding circumference was also initiated by Shanghai. This reform, which is very meaningful to the development of the service industry of China, received positive responses from some other big cities and the state administrations for finance and taxation. It is likely that this reform is going to accelerate the transformation of VAT to consumption-based VAT.

It is also very interesting to note some institutional innovations in Guangdong Province. One is that, in 2010, Zhu Xiaodan, then the municipal Party secretary of Guangzhou (now the provincial governor of Guangdong), proposed that the policy of "admittance if not forbidden" should replace the policy of "conditional admittance." They are now approved to carry out the pilot project of a loose commercial registration policy. Another example is that Shenzhen has set up the "NGOs without competent authorities," which are implemented throughout Guangdong and have created good effects. Some officials of the Ministry of Civil Affairs also believe that such practice is more beneficial than harmful. And then there is the election system of village self-governance. This system has its existing legal basis, but it is not properly implemented in most areas. The example set by Wukan Village of Guangdong Province may make it less resistive to popularize this policy.

Generally, many grass-root institutional innovations provide direction reminders and implementation experience for the overall reform, and even the innovations themselves have overall significance. We should earnestly support those innovations in order to better combine "top-down design" and grass-roots innovation and collaboratively push forward reform. Thus, China will definitely overcome the present difficulties and make greater achievements in a new and higher level.

7

It Is a Progressive Process to Reach the Other Bank:

Thinking About the Thirty-Year Reform in Terms of Transition Economics[1]

Fan Gang

Fan Gang

Doctor of economics, professor at Peking University and Graduate School of the Chinese Academy of Social Sciences; Included in the list of Young and Middle-aged Experts with Outstanding Contributions to China, with a major academic specialty of theoretical economics, and engaged in the studies of economics for a long time. Currently serving as Vice Chairman of the China Society of Economic Reform, Secretary-general of the China Reform Foundation, and Director of the National Economic Research Institute.

---

[1]This article is based on the record of the speech delivered by the author in Shanghai Jiao Tong University on 12 June, 2008. Its publication is authorized by the author after review by the author.

The Other Bank Is Known

If it is believed that some wordings in the past were transitional, then, with 30 years having passed, it is necessary to be assured today that we are transitioning to a market economy and we are going to establish the fundamental systems and rules for a market economy.

What is a system comprised of? Generally, it is believed to be comprised of an incentive mechanism, a restrictive mechanism, and then a set of rules. What is a system? It is a set of rules of behavioral patterns that constrain people's behaviors and reconcile the interest relationships between each other. A system can be formal, which is set out in writing and needs enforcement, and can be informal, in which behavioral patterns and behavioral restrictions, etc. are reflected through culture and some other aspects.

An unprecedented phenomenon occurred in the reforms of the Soviet Union and East Europe from the end of the 1980s to the beginning of the 1990s: people strived to transform the existing planned economy to another existing system, the market economy. The system reform at that time was one with a known goal — a market economy was already known to all. Hence transition economics emerged.

The goal for the Soviet Union and East Europe was very clear then: they wanted to return to Europe in 300 days or 500 days ("To return to Europe" remains the version used by East European countries even today), that is, to transform their systems into the system of the market economy of the Western Europe and the US. The European and American economic advisors proposed various programs for the Soviet Union and East European countries. The goal was very clear: to complete the transition in 300 days or 500 days. They said, you might go through the transition and make turns here and there.

Did China know the goal of reform in the very beginning? It was believed in the past that China did not know. If China did not know this goal, then the issue China faced was not one about transition, but rather change of the system.

Let's recall carefully: did we know or not? In the early days of reform, the circles of economic and political policies were greatly dedicated to the study of the goal of system reform, and a great compromise was made in the end. According to official documents, the earliest transition goal was proposed in the documents of the Third Plenary Session of the 11th Central Committee of the CPC. The official, yet somewhat obscure goal transition proposed then was to "combine the planned economy with the elements of commodity." But when we recall the whole process of the past thirty years, we'll find out that, for each step, the experiences of Hong Kong, of Singapore, and of America and Europe were learned by leaders and scholars. But it is impossible for us to "build Rome in a day." There were many compromises and changes to make. But we learned from references for each step, and for the next step, new references were taken for emerging problems. (If we believe the process of transition is a progressive process, we may find that there are many intermediate forms, and after each form there is going to be new problems).

One of the questions the leaders consulted the academics about the study must be: what did the others do about this? What did the countries practicing market economy do? What were the international rules? If you could not realize immediately, it meant that the transition could not be realized in a short term, but the goal for each step of the transition was there, consciously or unconsciously. The references were there and already known. The information might not be complete, but you know something anyway.

Then let's think about the famous saying of "crossing the river by feeling the stones." We had to cross the river but did not know how, so we had to feel the stones, but the goal of crossing the river was definite. Was it necessary to define what the river was? Not necessarily. It might be difficult to define the exact reason, but it was clear that we had to arrive at the other bank. We knew our system did not work, but we found another system in the world that worked more efficiently and we wanted to learn from them, so that's why we wanted to get to the other bank, which was clear. "Crossing the river by feeling the stones" means that the goal was known but not yet the path to get there.

If some ideas for the past were transitional, then, 30 years after, it is necessary for us to get a definite goal that we are going to transition to a market economy and establish the basic policies and rules of a market economy.

This market economy may be combined with Chinese characteristics, i.e. our culture and history, especially some culture and thinking that are concerned about the system, which have been developed over a long history. They will not affect the establishment of the basic systems needed for a market economy (e.g. property relations, checks and balances in the legal and political systems, and participation of interest groups). There could be diversified patterns, but the fundamental elements of the system must be in place — the transition should be realized through some fundamental institutional issues.

Reform Under the Constraint of Vested Interest

Compensation may indeed eliminate some conflict of interests and reduce some obstacles, but it is impossible for some conflict of interests to be eliminated by means of compensation. It is not a matter of speed for radical reform and progressive reform, but a matter of different ways of dealing with vested interest. For establishing a new system, it is not necessary for the radical reform to go very fast.

During the transition from a planned economy to market economy, none of the system patterns were coordinating and stable. You will find that nobody was satisfied with it. Further institutional reform must be carried out as long as the new interest group has constituted the majority.

After making clear that the past thirty years was a process of transition, and by knowing where the starting point is and where to turn to, the process is added to the agenda of study. It is found that there were generally two categories of problems during transition. The problems of the first category were about the unwillingness or impossibility of transition; the second category was about the incapability of transition, for everything would be brought to chaos if it was changed and they did not know how to change. By employing the economic wording, the process of transition is actually a process in which the old system is transitioned, under the constraint of vested interests and information incompleteness, toward a known system. There were two constraints in transitioning from a planned economy to market economy. The first constraint was produced by the old system. How did the old system constrain the transition? It was the obstacle from the groups with a vested interest. The second constraint is information incompleteness, which means when we try to find out what others do for each step, it is inevitable that we get confused about the relationship between different systems due to inadequate information.

We talk about "emancipating our mind" quite often now — the established ideology impeded the reform and, to reform, we need to emancipate our mind, as talked about by all in the past 30 years.

Ideology is a relatively independently factor that may be a determinant for the system in terms of institutional economics. According to Douglass North and some others, ideology may reduce the cost of institutional transformation. It may make people more selfless in calculating their own interest and only striving for the new system. The revolutionists and innovators who fight for new systems think less for their own benefit. What they want more is principle, justice, morality and fairness of society: because systems are public goods; they are not for private consumption, but for the consumption by the whole of society.

But China is not a country with strong ideology. China is not a religious country. There was no religious rule in China, and there was no war waged out of religion. In China, strictly speaking, it is not so convincing to take the ideological impediment as the impediment to reform as it was in the Soviet Union and East Europe. It was because of this that the Soviet Union failed to boost its economy; its political ideology impeded the economic development. This is not the case with China. China may choose to do something as long as there is a principle in place and do it in a flexible way. Emancipating the mind, to a great extent, is a process of getting flexible.

A more important problem for China is: the vested interest formed in the old system became the impediment and obstacle for the birth and development of a new system. System is a set of methods for distributing interests, and when a system is changed, it means the structure for interest distribution is changed. The essential part of the institutional transition is to change people's interest relationships and adjust the relationships between interest groups. There must be some interest groups which suffer losses and some which gain more, so we will see both of the groups supporting reform and also groups against the reform.

Reform is a non-Pareto improvement. Through Pareto improvement, at least one receives benefits while nobody suffers losses. It is impossible to make nobody lose in reform, so it cannot be a Pareto improvement (many people are confused with this concept). The problem for the past thirty years is not the one about economics, but the one of political economics. Political economics studies non-Pareto improvements, which is a process in which interest groups are involved in direct conflict. Pareto improvement cannot be realized by means of price mechanisms and market mechanisms. Therefore, the reform is full of conflicts, and sometimes enforcement.

For a long time, there has been a compensation theory in economics. Is not the problem solved when the benefited people compensate the losing part a bit, to make up for them by sharing some new interests out of the dividends of reform and the improved efficiency of the transition? We did try some methods of compensation, such as "non-staple food subsidies" in price reform and the compensation for laid-off workers.

It is true that compensation may eliminate some interest conflicts and reduce some impediments, but it cannot solve all problems. Some interest conflicts cannot be solved through compensation. First, we cannot compensate the privileged class. If you belonged to the privileged class in the past, your absolute income is not changed after reform and it might even increase. But your relative income decreases and you begin to feel lower in society. This cannot be compensated.

Second, if compensation equals restoration of the old system, this cannot be compensated either. If people only got paid without any effort in the past and now also get paid the same way as before without efforts, it means that the system has not changed. If people receive less payment without efforts, they might suffer a lot, and this impediment is also hard to get rid of.

Third, many things on the spiritual level cannot be compensated. For example, if the ideology changes and what one believes changes in reality, such spiritual loss cannot be compensated with material.

Fourth, some interests, like dividends of reform, are normally to be gained in a short term. In the short-term reform, we only pay costs. There might be some chaos in the beginning of reform, and then huge costs, which might cause a decline in the economy. It was most obvious in the Soviet Union and East Europe. There was decline in the economy overall and also people's income in the first years. The benefits of reform tend to be shown after five, ten, or twenty years since the reform is started. Then there will be conflict between short-term and long-term interests. Then there is no way for compensation. You are not able to compensate the present with future benefits.

The issue of getting loans for the reform was discussed then. If loans can be obtained somewhere in the world for a country's reform, the impediment for the reform would be smaller, because the loans can be used for giving salaries and ensuring the current interest, and the loans could be repaid once the dividends of reform are produced in the future. There were arguments about whether the World Bank could provide loans to the countries that would carry out reforms, but the problems of a large country such as China could not be solved merely through loans. Therefore, it was impossible to get rid of the impediment for reform caused by short-term interests. This explains why the older generations are prone to be conservative and against the reform, while the younger generations support the reform — younger people can wait to see the dividends of reform in the future, but the older generation cannot.

Yao Yang, a scholar from Peking University, is writing a book, trying to explain why China has succeeded in reform. He employs a term created by Mancur Olson, i.e. the "disinterested government," which does not work for itself, but for the interests of all citizens. In reality, any government has its particular interest in it, including elections, long-term administration, and even for more private purposes, the interests of their relatives, friends and themselves. He explains that if a disinterested government existed, it would be much easier for it to realize reform and realize the institutional transition aiming at the goal of interests of all citizens.

The real concern is not whether the government in reform is "disinterested" but whether the government is able to overcome some short-term interests and ensure their goals for long-term interests. Politicians or statesmen have their specific terms of office. If a political system may help them pursue some long-term interests rather than short-term interests, some impediments during the process of transition may be overcome and less short-term deformation will be brought to this system, and not let the short-term interests impede the long-term development. In the early period of transition, the most difficult could generally be how to pursue a long-term interest and whether a type of mechanism or political system should be created to maximize this type of long-term interest.

In dealing with interest relationships, there are two ways of tackling interest-based impediments for reform: radical reform and progressive reform, which differ in terms of approach rather than speed. The basic approach for radical reform is to enforce some measures (perhaps some compensation) regardless of the existence of vested interests, possible conflicts in society and the dissatisfactions of many people. In progressive reform, the transition is not realized radically but through progressive combinations. Some intermediate forms are implemented to also take care of vested interests, instead of immediately eliminating vested interests. It is a progressive transition. The latter is the typical way of transition in China.

Each generation has their own way. This is China's experience, or the so-called progressive reform. In the earliest days it was the dual-track approach to price reform. The old pricing was reserved and at the same time the free market was explored. The new demand was to be met by the market, and the original quota was still to be realized against the coupons. It was the incremental reform, in which the inventory was consumed bit by bit over time and the old system remained for a time. The inventory was to be consumed over a period of one generation or a certain period of time before the new system took shape based on the increment.

The most important part for reform is the increment. The new system will come into being to replace the old system once the increment begins. The most important thing is not how to reform the old things, but to develop a new system and new elements as soon as possible. A new system and new elements are always small at the start, but they will grow as long as they are superior. The most important part of reform is not the destruction of the old system, for the old system could be destroyed over night, but rather the establishment of a new system.

For China, the progressive reform means the incremental reform. The reform of each system means the increment, and besides, the incremental reform is also carried out in terms of regional development, that is, the special zones for economic development. In these piloting areas, an increment was formed in regional development, gradually breaking the old system.

There will be some transitional patterns in a progressive reform of system. The process will be very long. The radical reform may not necessarily be short in terms of length, as it is relatively quicker to break an old system, but it takes longer time to establish a new system. The establishment of any new system is a long process, during which there are always some intermediate forms and one such question: will a new interest group emerge during the reform which will impede the progress?

The most typical situation could be corruption. In every dual-track system, many make a profit, forming a new vested interest group. In various intermediate forms and in an incomplete legal system, the old system is not broken, so all types of corruptions arise. Will the emerging vested group become an impediment for reform? This is the question that has been repeated, constantly discussed and criticized over the past thirty years.

First, it is certain that some new interest groups will emerge during each period of institutional transformation and transition and in each system of intermediate form. But the basic theoretical way of thinking is: first, the target system is superior to the existing system; second, as said by Janas Kornai, the planned economy is a self-stabilizing and self-coordinating system, so is the market economy. But when a planned economy is transformed to a market economy, all the intermediate institutional forms are incongruous and unstable. You will find that nobody is satisfied with them.

I used to propose an idea of "reform anxiety." Oversees returnees and international consultants would say there is something wrong with this and that during the process of transition and they are not consistent with what is defined in textbooks. Someone having experienced the old system would think: the new system destroys my interest and I am not satisfied with it. As to the majority, even those with a vested interest, would think our interest is only transitional and temporary and it is to be changed anyway, and the best way is to maintain interest.

Nobody is satisfied with it, so it fails to reach a balanced, stable status. Therefore, it will still be on the track of change. Thus, the newly-formed vested interest group will certainly not be the interest group forming the majority. Besides, the vested interest group of the old system will not impede the reform by collaborating with the new vested interest group. They will, on the contrary, collaborate with the interest group continuing to welcome the reform and go against the interest group formed in the new system. The further reform of the system is inevitable politically as long as the new interest group does not constitute the majority.

The target being superior to the starting point means that the reform will not return toward the original point, but will roll on. There may be some twists and turns in the process, but people know that return will not do. So, although dissatisfied with the existing system and criticizing it, people have no choice but to go forward to the other bank of the river.

There are many problems now, such as corruption, widening wealth gap, an expanding low-income group, and so on. These are all issues about development. With the expanding of these problems, the force of the New Left becomes relatively stronger. Either the Libertarian or the Left are criticizing this system from various perspectives. The Left thinking is not held by some individuals; it reflects the trend of social thinking to some extent and the transitional status of this system, which is worthy of respect. This is a good phenomenon that people criticize from different perspectives. But a closer look will make us convinced that even the most conservative

Left and the most conservative groups will not propose to return to the original system, because everyone knows that it is not the right way.

Therefore, the analysis of the dynamic state of the reform shows that, despite the emerging vested interest group, the process of transition will go on, as long as we assume that: first, the target system is superior to the original system; second, the intermediate, transitional system is not stable.

Economy and Politics

Seen from the perspective of economic development, generally in the initial stage, there are comparatively more private goods, and there will be more public goods when the development goes on, and the politics is also playing an increasingly important role. This is what we have experienced in the past thirty years.

Religious doctrines and ideology are more binding to the Soviet Union, which means that no economic reform can be carried out unless the political and constitutional wordings were changed. We also changed some, but we did not have to change them all. We might choose to go ahead without a very clear goal.

With the increase of public goods, there must be more participation of interest groups and more checks and balances. The bigger the public finance is and the more the resources to be distributed by the government are, the more important are the issues of anti-corruption and interest checks and balances.

In terms of economics, politics is but an extension of economic activities — leaving out ideology, principles, concepts and morality, politics is a mechanism for distributing public goods. The whole economy is divided into two categories of goods: private goods and public goods. Private goods are allocated, distributed and transacted through the free market to realize resource allocation. Public goods, due to their high transaction cost and pricing cost, are provided by public means, including tax collection, public finance and provision of public goods, as well as the system, which is a kind of soft public goods. The original purpose of politics lies in these issues: it is a mechanism to reconcile interest conflicts in the process of supply. Once public goods are involved, however, there emerges the problem of abusing power for personal gains, so it is necessary to have a system of checks and balances.

There are two fundamental concerns of politics: the first is participation, and the second is checks and balances. By participation, it means that each interest group has to send a representative to take part in the distribution of public goods. What the congresses of western countries discuss all day long is not about ideology — the issues about socialism, capitalism and communism — but about public finance and public distribution, such as how much subsidies to be provided to the black, to women, to this state and that, and how much tax should be levied on the poor and how much on the rich. Each interest group has to participate in it.

The second is checks and balances. There should be checks and balances between each interest group, each political party, and each political faction. There should be checks and balances between each department with power, in order to prevent power abuse for personal gains and corruption. For the purpose of participation and checks and balances, it is necessary to have laws and a set of policies binding people's behaviors. This is the third concern for political reform. Therefore, the three concerns of politics, including participation, checks and balances, and policies, rules and laws, are all included in the scope of economics.

In terms of the relationship between the economy and politics, first, they are inseparable. Second, what economy involves first is the distribution of private goods. If there is independence between the supplies of private goods and public goods, it may be easier to carry out the reform of private goods and to establish the market for allocating private goods. There does not need to be big reform in society. Market will be formed as long as transactions are permitted. However, the reform of public goods is more difficult. Third, in terms of economic development, generally in the initial stage, there are comparatively more private goods, and there will be more public goods when the development goes on, and the politics is also playing an increasingly important role. This is what we have experienced in the past thirty years.

The right to transaction was first permitted in the rural reform 30 years ago, since the time when private goods developed. The "households with ten-thousand-yuan income" emerged, daily consumer goods were available to everyone, peasants got rich and the first thing they did was to build houses. as houses are private goods. For a long time in rural areas and some small towns, we found that the houses were beautifully built and well decorated, but there were no well-built roads. There were only muddy roads. There were no public goods. Entering the era of urbanization, public goods, the issue of pollution, the issue of social security, etc., became more and more important. After the people's basic demand for private goods is met, the demand for public goods (or at least half-public goods), including social security, medical treatment and education, become more and more important, and politics becomes more and more important. Therefore, seen from the course of economic development, for a developing country like China, it is natural to reform the areas of private goods in the first place, and then enter the areas of public goods. In recent years, the issues of government transformation and political reform have also been added to the agenda.

Of the political reform and economic reform as we often discuss about, which one serves as the premise? There is no definite answer to it, because different countries have different situations. According to the general principles of transition economics, the reform of the system concerning private goods is easier and may be carried out earlier. The reform of other areas may be carried out later due to wider coverage. So the reform of government was carried out later. But it is unfair to say that it is unnecessary for the political reform to serve as a premise to the economic reform. The Third Plenary Session of the 11th Central Committee of the CPC is a significant political reform, shifting the political line of the "Cultural Revolution" to the current political line. From the politics of isolation from the outside world to the politics of reform and opening up, it is a significant political reform, so it is not fair to say that China initiated the economic reform before the political reform.

The political reform of China at that time was not as pressing as the political reform of the Soviet Union. They had the religious tradition. Religious doctrines and ideology are more binding to the Soviet Union, which meant that no economic reform could be carried out unless the political and constitutional wordings were changed. We also changed some, but we did not have to change them all. We might choose to go ahead without a very clear goal.

The interest structure of China was very different from that of the Soviet Union and East Europe. At the start of reform, when the country had experienced the planned economy for 70 years, the economy of the Soviet Union stopped growing. Its interest structure was completely changed. The vested interest also stopped growing, so the vested interest group who wanted to protect the old system was becoming smaller and smaller. I attended a conference in Italy several days ago, and Gaidar was also there (he served as Prime Minister during Yeltsin's administration). He said, we initiated political reform and strived to construct democracy not because the westerners wanted us to, but because we ourselves wanted to do so. 80% of the votes were cast for Yeltsin. At that time, 80% of the population wished to undergo radical reform, to completely destroy the old political system, to return to Europe. It was not the propaganda that worked, but it was because there was such a foundation in the social structure of Russia.

The "Cultural Revolution" was a catastrophe to China's economy, but after the "Cultural Revolution" was ended in 1976, our economy grew at a rate of 10% each year in 1977 and 1978. There was no such complete revolutionary social foundation then. The vested interest was able to endure through the period. The economy was messed up by the "Cultural Revolution," so when the interest structure was relatively stable, everybody wished to immediately develop the economy. The economic reform could also be initiated even without a thorough political reform then.

Up to now when the reform has been ongoing for the past thirty years, it is natural for us to come to a conclusion: the political reform will be the focus for the next step, because it has come to this stage in a natural way. For the distribution of public goods, there must be more participation of interest groups and more checks and balances. The bigger the public finance is and the more the resources to be distributed by the government are, the more important is the issues of anti-corruption and interest checks and balances. So it is more necessary to bring the political reform to the agenda.

Corruption is a typical problem in transition, a problem occurring in the transitional period. Why is corruption such a serious issue in China? On the one hand, the development has created more and more public goods. On the other hand, many old systems remain unchanged, with many rights still public rights, which should have been transformed to private goods and private rights. But they remain public rights, resulting in overgrown public rights and creating the possibility of corruption.

There are altogether two types of rights and two types of benefits: public rights and private rights, and public benefits and private benefits. It is the government's and civil servants' responsibilities to gain benefits for the public by using public rights; to gain private benefits by using private rights, this is the instinct of individuals and private enterprises; to gain benefits for the public by using private rights, this is an altruism, like donating for the Sichuan Earthquake; but to gain private benefits by using public rights is corruption.

The foremost question is: why are there so many public rights? When there are so many public rights, which provides the possibility of corruption to so many people, corruptions cannot be brought under control and the responsible individuals be punished. It is said in economics that there is no free meal. It was proposed to supervise public rights and strengthen the oversight mechanism, but the proposal ended up with a supervisory committee and a committee which supervised the supervision. Some people even proposed to organize a supervisory committee which would supervise the "committee which supervised the supervision." Hong Kong needs only the Independent Commission against Corruption to deal with the problem, because the scope of public rights in Hong Kong is very small.

Therefore, the first thing we need to do is reduce public rights. Some people criticize that the dual-track reform provides the possibility of corruption, by which public rights can be monetized. In the past, some private benefits for using public rights could only include one bottle of

Maotai or one box of Chunghwa cigarettes, and now it could be ten bottles of Maotai, which could be sold if it cannot be consumed by the receiver. This is a small monetized case. Later, the direct money-giving could be boundless, as compared to those tangible gifts. This is a typical transitional problem. It is not a natural problem out of the reform, but a problem that remains unsolved. If we do not carry on with the reform, the transitional corruption will evolve into institutional corruption.

The Reform with Information Incompleteness

The second constraint on the transition is information incompleteness. There are three cases of information incompleteness. First we may probably know how a system is operated, but you do not know why it is operated that way and what are the details backing it. Second, you do not know how long it will take to establish a new system, such as the legal system. A draft should be prepared at first and ideas are presented in writing, then it will not get adopted before several rounds of discussions. But this is not yet the real system, because it is still necessary to formulate implementation rules, include cases and judicial precedents. When someone fails to enforce this law, he will be punished, and that's when the law begins to play an institutional role in reality and becomes a binding force and a rule to everyone. Third, you do not know how the institutional elements check and coordinate with each other.

When the stock market began to implement the reform of equity division, who would imagine these problems? The equity division itself is a transitional system, whose reform was under discussion for seven years (from the beginning of discussion) and the reform was ongoing for three years. After the reform, stock analysts came to find the problem of non-tradable shares in the end. Why did they forget this term when they induced stock investors last year? Non-tradable shares are not a new policy, are they? It is the rule which was established from the very beginning of the stock market reform. When investors were confident that the stock market was becoming the one with complete circulation, these people who advocated the reform began to ask the government to stop the policy of non-tradable shares and return to the past.

How long will it take from establishing a stock market to making one with an entire and complete circulation? We may probably get the answer now. But a securities market is only a link, an element, of this system, which is more or less known to us. But there is something you do not know or at least not know exactly.

I used the term of "frictional cost" in an article published in 1991. There is an option for decision-making between the efficiency and benefits gained from reform and the frictional costs paid for the reform. Kornai came up with a concept of "incoherence cost" in 1990. He argued that the transitional status in the process of reform was not incoherent in itself, and such incoherence would produce a lot of frictions and chaos, leading to a decline in the economy, etc. It was created to explain the phenomena of East Europe and the Soviet Union at that time. The radical reform caused social chaos, loss of efficiency, and decline in production. This type of frictional costs will definitely arise in economic reform.

In terms of information incompleteness, the difference between the progressive and the radical lies in how much risk you are willing to take on: do you take on the great incoherence costs in order to acquire fast institutional benefits? How much damage will this cause to the society? The reason for the Soviet Union and East Europe to choose this kind of line, in a sense, on the one hand, was because the aforesaid vested interest became smaller, and on the other, because they were able to pay high social costs as a country with high industrialization. Some of their basic systems of social morality, culture, knowledge and education had taken shape, so they could afford greater frictional costs without affecting the fundamental stability of society. It is hard to say about less developed countries. As least we have seen the chaos of them when the reform was initiated: they became "failed states" which were unable to supply basic public goods to society.

Frictional costs are reflected in different ways. The first is the so-called institutional bottleneck. The reforms of different systems are not in tune, meaning some reforms have been initiated while some are yet to happen, causing a bottleneck in the whole system, loss in efficiency, and creating social chaos. The second is the so-called proactive reform, meaning the reform of a certain area takes place much earlier than the other systems. There are counterparts to these two cases. It is more probable for China's problems to be a counterpart of the bottleneck problem. Ten years ago, the biggest bottleneck was the financial reform lagging behind the reforms of the enterprises and other market areas. Now the financial reform is advancing a bit, but the reforms of the production elements market, political system and government have become the new bottlenecks, and the opening degree for the capital markets and capital accounts might be a new bottleneck.

Did we encounter the proactive reform? It occurred in some areas, but was not visible. It is more obvious in some countries. The problems of some Southeast Asian countries as exposed in the financial crisis of Asia were exactly the results of unfavorable reforms of the legal system and government, when the financial market and the capital accounts were opened much earlier than the reforms of the regulatory systems. Since then, the international community discussed a great deal about a word, "progressive," meaning there is a sequence among the reforms of different systems, which should be prioritized according to the elements of the systems. The progressive reform means the reforms of various areas are carried out step by step, but there is some coherence between them to avoid frictional costs.

The "Transitional Hybrid"

Township enterprises and the stock market with equity division, for example, are intermediate forms during the transition. How shall we look on this type of status? As a transitional form under various constraints, it must have some defects and the reform should be carried on, but anyway, it is an approach under other restrictive conditions. This is the best approach of the transition for the third issue of political reform, hence the name of the "transitional hybrid." Different from general "hybrids," the practical issues for transition primarily include: how to increase the momentum for reform to solve the problem of interest frictions; and how to increase information to reduce frictional costs. Restricted by vested interest and information incompleteness, a set of intermediate forms arise during the transition. I called it the "transitional hybrid."

It is not a hybrid composed of something with specific constituents in it. It is not a hybrid car, but a variation, forming a special mechanism, a mechanism of transitional variation. There are several typical cases, such as township enterprises and the stock market with equity division, whose reforms have basically been fulfilled. In terms of the overall economy, our society is a "hybrid" one now, something existing in a transitional period.

How shall we look on these "transitional hybrids?" When township enterprises emerged, most economists did not take them seriously, and did not believe it was a good institutional pattern, because contrasted with existing patterns as defined in textbooks; they were neither public enterprises nor private enterprises and incurred many problems. But they came into being under the constraints of a set of other systems, and they changed all the time, due to various problems; it was collective in the beginning, and then became joint-stock cooperation, and completing the process of transitioning from public enterprises to market-economy enterprises after going through the reform of the joint-stock cooperative system over the two stages.

At that time, there were two groups of people holding different opinions on it around the world: one group criticized it, and the other group believed it was a new hope, a third road, which was neither public nor private. Neither group won the debate. It was right for those criticizing it, but they were also wrong. Under the conditions at that time, it was the optimal reform mechanism, and the problem was only that defects were exposed one after another before this form became transitioned step by step. Was it a good form? Yes, it was. Was it perfect? No, it was not. Was it a third road? No, it was only a transitional form rather than a steady one.

It was the same with the stock market. If the equity division was implemented then, when would China's stock market take a step forward?

When would the reform of equity, the reform of the enterprise joint stock system be carried out? It was hard to say. Under the institutional conditions and ideology, the equity division was the best form to establish a stock market. Several years later, when problems are found and then need to be reformed, it means the transition is completed.

It was the same with other areas when we look back. Currently, many of our systems are in an intermediate status. How shall we look on this status? It is a transitional form constrained by various conditions, so there must be some defects and it needs continuous reform, but it is also the optimal approach to reform transition under the constraint by other conditions. Hence I call it the "transitional hybrid." We should push forward the reform rather than merely criticize its defects.

Nobody is satisfied with it when it is still in the intermediate status, which means the "reform anxiety." This is a good thing. "Reform anxiety" is a drive for reform. When people are made to realize that there are always some problems, the reform will go on and on. Many problems will emerge then, so the public will be anxious about it. The reform anxiety results in many criticisms of the reform itself, which has been the situation for the most recent seven or eight years. People not only criticize the system itself, but also the reform, believing there is something wrong with it. The reform is still in the intermediate status and has not been fulfilled, so there must be some problems. It is actually a confusion of thinking when people turn to criticize the reform itself.

I do not deny the problems arising in the reform. But we have to clarify the problems, because the reform is still ongoing, so they should not be attributed to the reform. I do not think it is possible for the reform to establish a perfect system very soon.

It has been thirty years for the reform. Looking forward, how long will it take us to arrive at the other bank? There are many determinants and it is hard to provide a quantitative analysis. Let us have a review of the systems of the market economy of the West and the various legal and political systems. It was a long process from the start of development to complete systems. It was a twinge lasting for the whole of the 19th century. It was after the Progressive Movement in the beginning of the 20th century and the Great Depression of the 1930s in the US that the macro-economic system and social security system were finally established. By then, it had taken at least 100 years for the market economy system to be established in a step by step approach.

Of course, we do not need 100 years to do the same thing, because we have a system model and system target in place, but we still need forty or fifty years to finish the journey. During the thirty-year reform, we still struggled in the old system in the first several years, and it roughly takes 20 years for a truly new system to be formed, so forty or fifty years in total is a reasonable length. Of course, the improvement of systems is not a simple process; it is subject to various factors.

8

How Can China Avoid

the Middle-Income Trap?

Cai Fang

Cai Fang

Director and Research Fellow of the Institute of Population Studies, Chinese Academy of Social Sciences, and member of the Chinese Academy of Social Sciences, professor of the Center for Agricultural and Rural Development (CARD), Zhejiang University, Distinguished Research Fellow at Unirule Institute of Economics (Beijing), member of the Committee of Soft Science of the Ministry of Agriculture, and member of the Committee of Experts of the Ministry of Human Resources and Social Security. His research focuses on labor economics, population economics, and the theories and policies on China's economic reform, economic growth, income distribution, poverty, and the issues of agriculture, farmers and rural areas. His recent publications include the Report on China's Migrant Population, Between Confusion and Non-Confusion, etc.

demographic dividend disappears, the restraint on economic growth will be but the output potential, rather than the demand factors within a time period."

—Cai Fang

when China has passed the Lewis Turning Point and the demographic dividend began to disappear rapidly; these two aspects will be manifested as lower output potential in supply. If this problem is not considered from a long-term perspective, there will inevitably be false judgment regarding the macroeconomic situation from a short-term perspective. The economic cycle and the economic growth are not only closely associated with each other, exerting important impacts on each other, but are determined by different factors respectively. Therefore, the short-term and long-term perspectives should be combined to make correct estimates of the stages of the economic development and of the macroeconomic situation, and then to work out target policies and methods. If it is believed that the slowdown of economic growth is caused by cyclical factors, and measures are taken to boost economic growth from the perspective of demand, it is literally in the opposite direction. This tends to cause disastrous consequences as is shown in the experience of other countries. That is to say, the slowdown of economic growth deteriorates to economic retardation, which, in many cases, has dragged some countries into the middle-income trap.

This article is going to make an estimate about the change in China's economic development stages, and further to make an estimate of the macro economy from the long-term and short-term perspectives by summarizing the four steps of falling into the middle-income trap, in order to help readers become familiar with the problems and challenges faced by China's economy. It also provides a warning against making incorrect estimates concerning the development stages and the macroeconomic situation, and to further make specific policy suggestions on long-term sustainable growth.

Becoming Familiar with the Stages of China's Economic Development

In the early days of the reform and opening up, with the successful reduction of poverty on a large scale, China broke away from the Malthusian trap and entered the stage of developing a dual economy, having realized the

Lewis Turning Point and the arrival of the disappearing point of demographic dividend, China's economic development is currently facing a fundamental change, which is essentially the transformation from a dual economic growth to neo-classical growth. Whether China's economic growth miracle will come true will be determined by whether there is going to be a correct estimate of the stage of China's economic development and whether the nature of the challenges faced by China's economy can be understood. If a theoretical framework for combining the long-term and short-term perspectives is absent, it is very likely for us to make a paradoxical estimate and even produce mistaken policy conclusions when we are faced with a transformation for which there has been no experience to learn from.

A common method for defining the stage of China's economic development is to compare China with some economies which have experienced similar stages and have realized high income. For example, it is a very significant research topic, which, however, requires extra attention, to compare China with Japan. As with China, considered as a miracle-maker that surpassed other economies successfully, Japan has had a development path that is quite similar to China's in many respects. The similarities include the fact that the two countries have both benefited from the demographic dividend that has been created by demographic transformation into economic development and the fact that the governments of the two countries have both played a prominent and more direct role in economic growth. More importantly, however, China and Japan have both passed the Lewis Turning Point in which the labor supply changes from unlimited supply to shortages and passed the turning point where the demographic dividend disappears.

China is more similar to Japan of the 1960s and 1970s in terms of personal income per capita, from which a conclusion may be naturally drawn that, based on the experience of Japan, there is another 20 years even longer for China to grow at a higher rate. This conclusion of course helps people to better understand the possibility of China's economic growth, but

China is able to avoid the middle-income trap. In fact, rather than go through the middle-income stage successfully and become one of the high-income economies, many countries end up facing the economic retardation in the stage while still having growth possibilities, but end up in the middle-income trap. Therefore, it is more specific for China to locate the fundamental determinant for sustainable growth, rather than spot the possibility of keeping sustainable growth.

Although it is generally regarded that the Lewis Turning Point emerged in Japan's economic growth in 1960 when labor shortages and wage increases emerged, the disappearing point of the demographic dividend represented by the fact that the working-age population stops growing and the dependency ratio begins to rise did not occur until the early 1990s. In respect to the interval between the two turning points, China's "aging before affluence" was manifested in different ways. That is to say, it only took several years for the 15- to 64-year-old working-age population to stop growing in 2013 after the Lewis Turning Point was reached in 2004. Based on China's reality, if the 15- to 59-year-old population is defined as the working-age population, it began to decline notably from the emerging peak in 2010.

Therefore, it is more effective for us to compare the China of 2010 with the Japan of 1990 in order to reach the conclusion that the two countries were faced with similar challenges thus coinciding with the original purpose of the comparative study. It was in 1990 that Japan's economic bubble burst, wherefrom its economic growth was caught in retardation for over 20 years. For example, during the period from 1990 to 2010, the average growth rate of Japan's GDP was only 0.85%. In order to understand the severe challenges China is presently faced with, it is useful for us to observe what kind of similar changes Japan encountered at that time and how those changes were related to the "lost 20 years" of Japan's economy.

In the typical dual economic development, labor is supplied unlimitedly, and the labor needed for the economic growth that is limited by the industrial accumulation capacity may be supplied at an unchanging wage at accompanied by the transfer of labor from rural areas to cities on a large scale. In terms of this process, China differs greatly from Japan in several aspects.

First, China's labor flow has always been faced with very big institutional obstacles. Before the reform and opening up, strictly restricted by the policies of the people's commune, planned purchase and marketing by the State, and registered households, the transfer of surplus rural labor was delayed for decades. Even after the start of the reform and opening up, China has still been restricted by the registered household policy while the labor flow has been expanding continuously on a larger scale and on a wider scope. So it is fair to say that the labor transfer is not over, because the transferred labor and their family members have failed to become permanent urban residents; it remains a model of "ongoing flow."

Second, the period of reform and opening up is also the process in which China's population is undergoing rapid transformation at a speed much faster than other countries, thus becoming characteristic of "aging before affluence." Therefore, China will welcome the disappearing point of demographic dividends soon after the emergence of the Lewis Turning point, which is different from Japan's 30-year interval between the Lewis Turning Point and the disappearing point of demographic dividends.

In arguing about whether China is reaching its Lewis Turning Point, it is suggested that the "Lewis Turning Period" replaced the "Lewis Turning Point," in light of the long-term economic development stage whose change is also reflected in a specific time period. We believe that, based on the experience of other Asian economies, the interval between the Lewis Turning Point and the disappearing point of demographic dividends is a transition period for easier observation.

Fig. 1 shows the whole course in which China's working-age population aged between 15 and 59 changes from rapid growth to slower growth, to zero growth, and then to negative growth. Generally, accompanied by this change in the working-age population, the dependency ratio undergoes a course in which it drops rapidly and then at a lower speed, and then rises

population represents these two courses. As is shown in the figure, the year 2004 is marked as the Lewis Turning point and the year 2010 is marked as the disappearing point of demographic dividends, and the time period between 2004 and 2010 is the Lewis Turning Period.

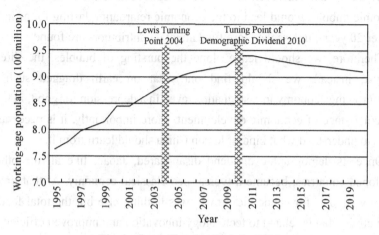

Fig. 1   Lewis Turning Period of China
Source: China Development Research Foundation, China Development Report 2011/12: Changes of Demographic Conditions and Resulting Policy Adjustment, China Development Press, 2012.

According to the theory of the dual economy, when the labor demand grows faster than the growth of the labor supply, which leads to the disappearance of unchanging wages during the period of typical dual economic growth, the first Lewis Turning Point emerges. With the emergence of migrant-worker shortages and the following continuous wage increases as the empirical evidence in 2004, China reached its Lewis Turning Point. In 2010, the working-age population reached its peak, which was followed by the negative growth. Correspondingly, the dependency ratio began to rise after touching the bottom, meaning the total disappearance of the demographic dividend. Affected by the characteristic of "aging before affluence," the Lewis Turning Period in China was rather short, lasting for only 6 years.

that its Lewis Turning Period was from 1960 to 1990. The economy of Japan kept growing at a high speed for these 30 years, and after that, the economic growth of Japan stopped abruptly. It seemed that Japan experienced the economic bubbles in the 1980s, since the economic growth has not recovered so far. However, it is hard to believe that the bursting of the economic bubbles would lead to the economic retardation lasting for as long as over 20 years, unless the more fundamental contributors are found.

Therefore, we should leave alone the bursting of bubbles, the direct catalyst; instead, we should find out what on earth dragged such a rapid-growing economy into stagnation, even in a depression for good, in that particular stage of economic development. More importantly, it is necessary for us to understand what kind of lesson China should learn from it.

Once its demographic dividend disappeared, Japan, like all the other developed countries, became a typical neo-classical economy. At that time, the only support for economic growth was nothing else but the total factor productivity that is related to technology innovation and improved efficiency of resource distribution. The key for Japan's economy to realize an appropriate growth rate lies in whether the improvement of the total factor productivity is kept at the same level with the other developed countries. It shall be determined by various factors, including the institutional dynamics, innovation capability and labor capital level. Japan indeed had some fundamental barriers in these aspects.

For example, protecting lifeless enterprises prevented the redistribution of resources, and the intentional hold-up of higher education delayed the labor capital in fitting into the new development stage. In particular, facing the inevitable slowdown of the potential growth rate, the government used to focus on the investments driven by industrial policies and took a long-term and normalized approach to stimulating macroeconomic policies, trying to increase the economic growth rate in a demand-driven way, but the result was the opposite.

The working-age population aged 15–59 reached its peak in 2010 and the corresponding dependency ratio dropped to the bottom, China was faced which was primarily represented by the disappearance of the demographic dividend and the decline of the potential growth rate.

First, the labor shortage and the wage increase arising from it will notably and more and more severely weaken the relative advantages of the labor-intensive industries. The most remarkable features of the development of a dual economy are unlimited labor supply and wages always at the sustenance level for a long time. Therefore, the arrival at the Lewis Turning Point means continuous wage increases caused by the shortage of ordinary laborers, and it becomes notable for it to weaken the comparative advantages of labor-intensive industries. Since the high-speed growth in the past 30 years relied significantly on the demographic dividend of cheap labor costs, the disappearance of the demographic dividend will undoubtedly hold up the effects produced by the economic growth rate.

Second, facing the situation of ongoing wage increases, the simplistic attempt of raising wages and replacing manpower with machines will lead to the progressive decrease of a capital return. In light of the slowdown of the growth rate, the government tends to adjust the industrial policies and spur the growth, including encouraging and providing subsidies to emerging industries. As a result, the prices of capital elements will be distorted, which will not only directly facilitate the overly rapid growth of capital-intensive industries, but also induce enterprises to replace manpower with machinery and cheaper capital. The neo-classical growth is characteristic of, however, the inevitable progressive decrease of the capital return under the condition that labor is no longer supplied on an unlimited basis. The problem is that a growth rate that fails to bring about progress in productivity will not last long.

Finally, with the decrease of the rural working-age population and labor being transferred from the agricultural sector at a slower speed, the speed at which the efficiency of resource redistribution gets improved will slow down, making it even harder to improve the total factor productivity. Although the sources of improving the total factor productivity are still available, the existing institutional restraints, like the registered household labor, from flowing freely between enterprises, ownerships, sectors, regions, and the urban areas and the rural areas, which makes it harder to further improve the efficiency of resource redistribution.

In such circumstances, the change in the development stage alone, even if there is no misguidance in policies, will necessarily mean that China's economy will grow with a low output potential. We may observe the impact of this kind of change in the economic development stage on the economic growth rate by estimating the potential GDP growth rate. The potential growth rate is the normal economic growth rate that may be realized under the condition that capital and labor are fully utilized, with the restraint of the supply of certain production factors and within the limit to the increase of total factor productivity. Primarily due to the negative growth of the working-age population since 2010, we have made an estimate that, based on necessary assumptions, China's potential growth rate, which was 10.5% on average during the "Eleventh Five-year Plan," will drop to 7.2% during the "Twelfth Five-year Plan" and 6.1% during the "Thirteenth Five-year Plan."

How Does the Middle-Income Trap Emerge?

When China is still in the stage of above-average income, its demographic dividend disappears, i.e. at the turning point of the traditional economic growth whose source is being dried up. Although it is a natural stage of economic development, which does not mean that China is inevitably going to fall into the middle-income trap, such potential risk indeed exists, according to the experience and lessons of a great number of countries in the history of the world economy.

For example, some economists measure the economic level of each country with how much their GDP per capita accounts for in the GDP per capita of the United States. Therefore, the countries with a percentage over 55% are defined as high-income economies, those with a percentage of 20%–55% as middle-income economies, and those with a percentage below 20% as low-income economies. Of the 132 countries listed for such

2008. It is found, by observing the characteristics of change in this group, that it is possible for around half of the middle-income countries to remain in the same stage even after nearly half a century, and that the countries exiting the middle-income group will mostly flow downward to the low-income group; very few "graduate" and enter the high-income group.[1]

We may, based on the logic of economic analysis, integrate relevant factors, observe the respective causality, find something regular and universal in them, and differentiate among them so as not to repeat the same mistakes made by other countries. In other words, the middle-income trap has something in common with the poverty trap, i.e. both being a kind of equilibrium trap, a kind of equilibrium status that is too stable to be broken by any ordinary force; nevertheless, there are differences between the two — if the poverty trap is taken as the extension of a long-term Malthus status and it is usually hard to find the direct cause for this status, then it is fair to say that the middle-income trap is generally caused by some visible policy faults.

Therefore, we may construct a causal circle for the middle-income trap by referring to the policy faults of different countries in the process of economic development, in order to see what are the inevitable steps for falling into the middle-income trap and what contributes to the fact that a country is unable to escape from this kind of vicious circle, with which it will be simpler for us to locate the starting point for breaking the causal chain.

The first step: the rapid economic growth slows down in a specific period of the middle-income stage. For a late-comer, it is normally easy to realize a high growth rate in the development stage of transitioning from the poverty trap to the middle-income level through capital accumulation and labor investment. However, to a certain development stage, or where the previous source for growth disappears or there is some policy fault, the

---

[1] Prema-Chandra Athukorala and Wing Thye Woo, "Malaysia in the Middle-Income Trap", paper prepared for the Asian Economic Panel Meeting at Columbia University, New York City, March 24-25, 2011.

economies in the world, some scholars have found that, if calculated with the GDP (PPP) and the US dollar for 2005, when the GDP per capita reaches USD 17,000, the rapid growing economy tends to suffer a notable slowdown, normally by 2%.[1]

The second step: in the case of a drastic slowdown in economic growth, if there is any misunderstanding of the nature of the problem, the corresponding policies tend to be working in the opposite direction, even causing man-made distortions and making the slowdown become retardation. For example, if the slowdown is caused by low output potential and the government's policies are still focused on spurring the growth rate by expanding demand, a series of distortions and unfavorable results will be caused. The most serious distortion would be nothing else but in the government's abuse of industrial policies, resulting in distorted prices of production factors; and the most serious consequences out of such policies would be inflation, bubble economy, excess production capacity and improper protection of backward industries and enterprises. If so, the slowdown that could have been normal or temporary would be changed to a long-term slow growth or retardation.

The third step: facing a series of social problems brought about by economic growth retardation, the government deals with the problems through seeking temporary relief regardless of the consequences, leading to the overall distortion of the economic and social systems. For example, when the economic growth retards and the "cake" cannot be made bigger, the redistribution of the "cake" will form the common rent-seeking incentive in society, leading to increasing corruption. Due to the fact that the groups with privileges tend to have a bigger income and the Matthew Effect in income distribution, the income distribution deteriorates, which would in turn intensify social conflicts. At that time, the hard-up government generally could do nothing but resort to the Populism policy which can be

---

[1] Barry Eichengreen, Donghyun Park and Kwanho Shin, "When Fast Growing Economies Slow Down: International Evidence and Implications for China", NBER Working Paper, No. 16919, 2011.

harm the incentive mechanism in economic activities.

The fourth step: the unequal distribution of resources and income which come along with the economic growth retardation develop the vested interest group, who would try their best to maintain the distribution structure which is beneficial to them. Therefore, the system suffers a lot from long-term accumulation of defects which do no good to break the middle-income trap. Once the system is caught in this situation, relevant economic and social policies would be controlled by the vested interest group, which would not only cause economic growth retardation, but make it harder for the system to transform, thus reinforcing the system that is disadvantageous to economic growth. Accordingly, the production factors are no longer based on the principle of highest productivity, but the principle of maximizing the vested interest. The worst thing would be that not only is it impossible for a country to break away from the middle-income trap, but it might even go backward to the low-income level, once it is caught in such a situation.

There is indeed the causality between the above-listed steps chronologically and logically, so it would be the most effective to cut off the possibility of a vicious spreading in terms of logic; however, the phenomenon manifested in each step may coexist, so the relevant measures should be worked out in a comprehensive way. Based on the experience of some countries, before the slowdown in economic growth and retardation, the institutional defects that are harmful to sustainable growth are manifested generally, and the deterioration of income distribution also tends to harm the economic growth itself.

Becoming Familiar with the Macroeconomic Situation

Based on the correct estimates of the stages of economic development, we need to combine the features of long-term supply factors with the short-term demand factors in a macro-economy before we can correct estimates of the economic situation, thus to make further proposals regarding the decisions economy will also be faced with a short-term supply impact, such as the impact of the oil crisis in the early 1970s on some developed economies, but generally speaking, the potential growth rate determined by supply factors is stable in the long run; supply factors also feature its long-term trend, but it tends to fluctuate in the short run.

Therefore, only the combination of the long-term and short-term perspectives features the theoretical consistency and the practical transparency and leads to a correct conclusion and target policy choices in judging the macroeconomic situation. The close combination of the two is not only helpful in making a judgment of the macroeconomic situation, but also the precondition for working out correct policies and measures. Long-term supply factors and short-term demand factors contribute to four macroeconomic situations through different combinations.

The first situation is the combination of strong supply and strong demand, i.e. a strong output potential is matched with a high demand level. Generally, this mostly happens in the economic development stage where there is sufficient supply of production factors and no notable progressive reduction of income. So this is a kind of catching up in the dual economic development. In this situation, which is comparatively simple, there is not going to be a lasting cyclical unemployment, nor serious inflation.

The second situation is the combination of strong supply and weak demand, i.e. a strong output potential cannot be matched with a weak demand capacity. Most typical of this situation is that the cyclical demand impact disables the growth rate to reach the output potential level when an economic decline or financial crisis occurs during the process of catching-up. Normally, such combinations lead to a serious labor market impact and cyclical unemployment.

The third situation is the combination of weak supply and weak demand, i.e. a weak output potential is matched with a weak demand capacity. Generally, it is the situation in which the source for normal growth will fade away and the new growth source is not yet available when the stage of the dual economic development comes to an end. It is the normal state of a

The fourth situation is the combination of weak supply and strong demand, i.e. a weak output potential cannot be matched with a strong demand capacity. This kind of situation will not happen unless there is intentional policy interference, that is, the distorted policies are used to promote investments or expand exports. In the case of weaker output potential, if exuberant demand factors are stimulated intentionally, the actual growth rate will surpass the potential growth rate, and will produce such consequences as inflation, excess production capacity and even economic bubbles.

In fact, the theoretical situations out of the combination of supply and demand factors as mentioned above correspond to the macro economy in history and in reality. We may be able to understand the past, know the present, and foresee the future by means of this theoretical abstraction.

The first situation refers to the normal state of China's economy before the Lewis Turning Point prior to 2010. During that period, thanks to the demographic dividend attributable to the demographic transformation, the supply factors facilitated the economic growth and China's economy featured a high potential growth rate. For example, the potential growth rate between 1978 and 1995 was 10.3% on average; the potential growth rate between 1995 and 2009 was 9.8% on average. Meanwhile, the increase of residents' income, the rapid growth of investments and substantial export growth provided the corresponding demand factors. Therefore, a balance for the macro economy was formed at a high growth rate during this period on the whole (see Fig. 2). The growth rate gap which is represented with the difference between the potential growth rate and the actual growth rate, though fluctuating over years, has varied very sharply on the whole and is becoming smaller as shown in Fig. 2.

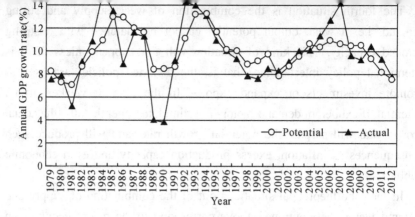

Fig. 2 Growth rate gap during the reform and opening up

Source: Cai Fang and Lu Yang, "Population Change and Resulting Slowdown in Potential GDP Growth in China", China & World Economy, Vol. 21, No. 2, 2013, pp. 1-14.

The second situation is the status in which there were severe internal or external impacts along the trend in the first situation. Since the middle of the 1990s, the domestic macroeconomic depression and the financial crisis in Asia had successively caused serious demand shrinking and underuse of production capacity, and then mass unemployment. After that, with China's entry into the WTO, the economic growth rate bounced back to the output potential level and the macro-economy recovered to the normal state, i.e. the first situation, by taking advantage of the overseas demand. Moreover, the inflation and the governance and adjustments after that from 1988 to 1989, as well as the global financial crisis from 2008 to 2009, dragged the actual growth rate below the output potential level.

The year 2012 was typical for the third situation. From the launch of the "Twelfth Five-year Plan" in 2011, the potential growth rate of China dropped significantly. Based on our estimate, the potential growth rate for 2012 dropped to 7.5% from 8.1% in the previous year. In such a circumstance, the notable decline in external demand happened to contribute to the matching between demand and supply. Therefore, the actual growth cause inflation. The actual growth rate did not fall below the potential growth rate, so there was no employment shock; on the contrary, the economic growth became more balanced.

The primary risks in China's economic growth in the future lie in the fourth situation, if any. There is a misunderstanding both held by economists and practitioners, who believe that the key determinant for economic growth lies in demand. As a result, it is most common that countermeasures are mostly targeted at some means for expanding domestic demand every time there is any barrier in economic growth. In the case of China, actually, it is somewhat reasonable to hold such an opinion since the middle of the 1990s, i.e. in the period when the shortage economy transformed to the surplus economy. However, once the economic growth passes the Lewis Turning Period and the demographic dividend disappears, the restraint on economic growth will be but the output potential, rather than the demand factors within a time period.

Considering both the development stage and the recent situation of China's economy, a conclusion may be drawn that the real challenge faced by China's economy is not the short-term macroeconomic demand factors, but long-term sustainability of economic growth. Put in another way, it is an incorrect option to go beyond the potential growth rate by stimulating demand. The correct policy option would be to improve the potential growth rate itself. However, if we persist in claiming that insufficient demand causes weak growth in theory and stick to various policy methods targeted at stimulating demand in practice, it is very likely that the problem will become a lasting reality and bring disastrous consequences. We might as well look back at the lessons learned by Japan in respect to this issue.

For a long period of time, it was generally believed throughout Japan that the high-speed economic growth of this country largely relied on overseas market demand, while the domestic consumption demand remained weak. Therefore, labor-intensive industries lost their advantages immediately after Japan passed its Lewis Turning Point in 1960; subsequently, it lost the demographic dividend in 1990, the high-income stage, where it was economic growth, while the government tried in every way to expand the domestic demand by taking various measures, including industrial policies, expansive fiscal policies and easy monetary policies. Presently, the so-called "Abenomics" characteristic of easy monetary policy follows this policy tradition.

The logic between the theory and the policy is in fact completely wrong. First, some effective research demonstrates that the consumption demand served as a driving force for growth that cannot be ignored when Japan's economy grew at a high speed, whereas the excellent export performance was the result of economic growth, rather than the cause. Second, there is other research which shows that the economic retardation of Japan after 1990 has been the direct consequence of the bad performance of its total factor productivity.[1] It was due to the misguidance from the aforesaid theory and policy, which led to incorrect "policy prescription," that Japan's economy has suffered the ill consequences over the past 20 years plus: economic bubbles and its bursting, widespread zombie enterprises and zombie banks, and economic retardation for as long as 20 years, one after another.

Conclusion and Policy Suggestions

In the circumstances that the demographic dividend disappears and there is a decline in the potential growth rate, if it is assumed that the other conditions remain unchanged, this does not mean that China will necessarily fall into the middle-income trap. After all, the demographic dividend is only the economic growth source in a particular development stage. It is only when it is replaced with a new source of productivity advancement that the dual economy may shift to the neo-classical growth and make the transition to the high-income stage. In fact, when the window for the demographic dividend is closed, the door to a more sustainable economic growth is opened instead,

---

[1] Fumio Hayashi and Edward C. Prescott, "The 1990s in Japan: A Lost Decade", *Review of Economic Dynamics*, 2002, 5(1):206-235.

One of the purposes of dividing the economic development into different stages is that late-comers may learn from the experience and lessons of the forerunners and then find a more successful way as early as possible. We should plan ahead by focusing on the following aspects based on the above-summarized steps for a country to fall into and get caught in the middle-income trap, as well as the reality of China's economic growth.

For the present, the most important thing for China is to have a correct understanding of the slowdown of economic growth, find the effective prescription, and reach a consensus between economists and decision-makers. In 2012, when the drop of the potential growth rate initially emerged, some misguiding opinions were prevalent among the public and within the academic circle. Almost everyone attributed the cause to insufficient consumption, forming the tendency of seeking "new economic growth points" for quite a time. The proposals included acceleration of urbanization, stronger investment in the infrastructure construction in the central and western regions, up-front investment in emerging industries, etc. from a long-term perspective. Sometimes, someone suggested stimulating macroeconomic policies, for they became confused between the long-term structural problems and the short-term cyclical problems.

These suggestions were not only based on incorrect estimates about the economic development stage and the macroeconomic situation, but they may also lead to particular risks. That is to say, it is very possible for these kinds of suggestions to fit easily into the policy meanings that the government is good at. The purposes of promoting urbanization, regional development strategies and industrial polices are correct policies in nature, with which the government has mature policy instruments and implementation approaches, or is familiar with, and obtained some good results in the past. Once they are used to drive the investment demand in order to reach the target of reaching and surpassing the potential growth rate, however, the opposite effect will be produced. The inevitable results would include deviation from the comparative advantages, greater surplus productivity, inflation and even asset bubbles, causing harm to the

The potential growth rate, in its original connotation, refers to the normal economic growth rate that can be realized under the conditions of the supply of production factors that are determined by resource endowment and on the basis of improved productivity that is determined by a series of other factors. So, with such means as administrative orders, media play-up and material incentives which are intended to drive the athlete's record above his/her athletic potential, it might be effective for a time to surpass the potential growth rate by demand-driven means, but it would cause injury to the athlete.

Similarly, as with the athletic training which is not perfect, there are some defects in the system that determine the supply of production factors and the improvement of productivity, which allows much room for us to improve the potential growth rate from the perspective of supply. Therefore, when the topic of creating policy dividend through reform is mentioned, it essentially means that policy conditions for better supply of production factors and improvement of productivity are created through reform, in order to reach the target of raising the potential growth rate. In other words, it means that the further improvement in the system of the socialist market economy may bring new sources and drive for China's economic growth.

Based on a model targeted at the potential growth rate, the change of at least two variables may increase the future potential growth rate substantially. And the two variables may lead to favorable changes through deepening the reform of the economic system.

First, if, during the period from 2011 to 2020, the non-agricultural labor participation rate is increased by 1%, the annual GDP potential growth rate on average for this period may be increased by 0.88%. In case of negative growth of the working-age population, there is still a method to increase the labor supply, that is, to increase the labor participation rate. The potential of increasing the labor participation rate comes from relevant reforms. For example, the transferred rural labor's employment in urban areas may be stabilized through promotion of the reform of the registered household system; more jobs may be provided through development and improvement

Second, if, during the period from 2011 to 2020, the total factor productivity is increased by 1% in the annual average rate, the annual GDP potential growth rate on average for this period may be increased by 0.99%. There are many approaches to improving total factor productivity. For instance, if the rural labor still accounts for a big percentage, the promotion of ongoing transfer of surplus labor may continuously allow for higher efficiency for resource redistribution; and the efficiency for resource redistribution may be improved also by creating a fairer competition environment, allowing production factors to flow freely among industries, sectors and enterprises, thus to let the enterprises with low efficiency for a long time exit the business and the efficient enterprises grow accordingly.

In addition, the improvement of the human capital of laborers will undoubtedly help the potential growth rate increase significantly. The approaches to human capital accumulation include various education and trainings, as well as "learning by doing." The incentive, quality and effects of education and training, as well as their ability to fit into the labor market, are all related to a series of institutional factors, which will raise further requirements on the reforms in the educational system, registered household system, public employment service, etc. respectively.

9

A Top-Down Design Is Urgently Needed for Political System Reform

Chen Jiagang

Chen Jiagang
Doctor of law. Currently working as a researcher for the China Center for Comparative Politics and Economics, and the Central Compilation & Translation Bureau. His professional field and research directions are: theories of politics, contemporary politics of China, and the study of Chen Duxiu. Organizing the translation of "A Collection of Translated Works on Consultative Democracy," and introducing the theories of "consultative democracy." Representative works include Consultative Democracy and Contemporary Politics of China, etc.

Deng Xiaoping pointed out in 1980 that, in order to meet the demand for democracy in the political life of the Party and the state and promote the beneficial and abolish the harmful, it was imperative to reform "the leadership system of the Party and the government." Then in 1986, Deng pointed out again, "Each step forward in economic reform has made us realize the necessity of political system reform. If we do not reform the political system, it will become impossible for us to guarantee the fruits of the economic system reform and keep it going, and there will be obstacles to the development of productivity and the four modernizations." As the chief designer of China's reform and opening up, Deng Xiaoping not only pushed forward the reform and opening up of China's society with his great courage, superior wisdom and rich experience, but also foresaw, in a rational way, the great significance of the reform of the political system to China's future development. These arguments still represent the glory of his wisdom, even today. At the press conference for the National People's Congress and the People's Political Consultative Conference on March 14, 2012, Premier Wen Jiabao pointed out, "Now the reform has come to the key stage. Without the success of political system reform, it will be impossible for the economic system reform to succeed, and it is even possible for the acquired fruits to be lost." The practice of China's reform and development has proved that it is necessary to promote the political system reform with a "top-down design" and in a comprehensive way. Each Party member, leader and cadre with the sense of responsibility should have a strong sense of urgency.

Since the start of the great cause of reform and opening up at the Third Plenary Session of the 11th Central Committee of the CPC in 1978, China has made remarkable achievements in socialist modernization construction, having made unprecedented breakthroughs in the construction of each area: economy, politics, culture, society, ecology, and the Party. The achievements made in economic construction are exceptionally marvelous. In political construction, however, it seems that the progress has been slow and lagging, and has even become an excuse of the western countries for criticizing and rebuking China. In fact, China has made particularly outstanding achievements in reform and development of the political system, entailing far-reaching significance, within the 90 years after the Chinese Communist Party was founded, within the 60-plus years after the People's Republic of China was founded, and within the 30-plus years after the reform and opening up was launched. The achievements of the political system reform can be summarized as follows: The ideas of democracy, rule of law, human rights, fairness, justice, respect and felicity have been very familiar to people, and tremendous changes have taken place in the area of political ideology; the authority of the constitution and laws are being established step by step and the guidelines of governance by law is taking shape; democracy within the Party is steadily progressing, and the developmental path for it is becoming increasingly clear, that is, that democracy within the Party promotes the democracy of the people, thus to actively promote grassroots democracy and improve consultative democracy; the tenure system for leaders and cadres has been abolished, and the substitution of members of the Party and government authorities will be gradually standardized and systematized; the political decisions will better fit the benefits and wishes of the people by stressing science and democracy instead of prior experience; the construction of a service-based government, rule-of-law government, transparent government and responsible government is being pushed forward energetically, and the government management system is being improved; society's self-government capacity is being strengthened and a vigorous citizen society is taking shape; the political life is getting more and more rational, systematic, standardized, and routinized; the rule of law is being better implemented on the system of power checks and oversight, and the power abuse and corruption has been considerably checked; and a citizen and political culture that is open, orderly, tolerant and rational is taking shape.

Nevertheless, if we always keep sober and calm, ready to listen to the opinions and suggestions of the public and courageous in facing realistic problems and hardships, we will realize that there is a long way to go for China's reform of political system. In terms of political system reform, we need more courage and wisdom, more plans and designs, more open minded and broader vision, more practices and implementations. It is necessary for us to follow the trend and logic of the development of history, become adapted to the built-in requirements of the development of economic life, push forward the political system reform in an overall way through "top-down design," and realize new breakthroughs.

Only through "top-down design" and overall reform of the political system can we meet the needs of developing the socialist market economy, effectively remove the impediments, pressures and bottlenecks of economic development, and win the victory for the key stages of economic reform. Since the reform and opening up, the socialist market economy system is being built through further pushing forward the transformation of government functions, clarifying the property ownership system, and actively playing the fundamental role of a market in resource distribution. However, the economic reform is presently entering the "deep-water area" in the reforms of the fiscal, tax and financial systems, income distribution system, price system, ownership system, state-owned enterprises, contractual relationships and good faith; with each step forward, the reform is faced with more pressure and bottlenecks in the political system. The government controls too many resources but checks the role of the market, and power and capital are combined to form vested interests, which have become the greatest challenge to the construction of an economic system. It is imperative to carry out political system reform and social reform in developing and perfecting the socialist market economy.

Only through "top-down design" and overall reform of the political system can we avoid the fragmentation of reform, that is, the benefits of reform are divided among departments, the benefits of the departments are divided among individuals, and the individual benefits are legalized. Reform is not a business only for yesterday, today, or tomorrow; reform is to be continued through the whole historical process of the socialist modernization construction. "Reform is always in the progressive tense; it will never be in the perfect tense," reform is not the business of one political party, one group or one department, but rather the business of the whole country and the whole nation; reform is not subject to any arbitrary policy, regulation, discovery or an innovation, but rather has its direction, goal and path. The reform is normal, healthy, integral and systematic and is in the interest of the people only when there is an overall design of reform on a strategic level, the constraints of old concepts are gotten rid of, and active exploration is permitted.

Only through "top-down design" and overall reform of the political system can we reasonably construct a reducing valve for the society, in order to facilitate expressing ideas, relieving pressure, overcoming controversies, eliminating conflicts, settling disputes, and remaining stable. The economic system reform has created huge benefits to the whole society, but it must solidify the benefits, which forms the vested interest that prevents the reform and provokes and exposes various controversies and conflicts. Various problems provoked by economic development and social transformation, including the problems with the economic structure and development approach, social conflict and opposition, wealth gap and corruption, declining public trust, mass disturbance, alienation from the people, and deteriorating ecology, etc., are common in the social life and cause ongoing problems for the reform process. We attend to one thing and neglect another. The justness of the existing systems is more often questioned, and the "legality of the administration performance" is severely challenged. The problems provoked and formed by economic reform cannot be solved only by the means of economic reform; it is particularly necessary to carry out the reform of the social and political systems in an integral and comprehensive way.

Only through "top-down design" and overall reform of the political system can we actively take part in global governance and energetically promote the construction of the new structure of a global economy and politics. Global development has changed the structure of global governance. Such issues as global energy safety, financial crisis, climate change, environmental problems, epidemics and terrorist activities pose threats to the whole human race. As a large developing country, China is more deeply involved in the international community and takes part in international politics more often so as to play a bigger role in the world, which already has become a trend. However, it is far from enough to merely win respect and have influence in modern international affairs by providing economic aids and debt reduction. In order to play a dominant role in the international community, it is necessary to follow the mainstream value of the international community, and develop an overall strategy that is fit for self-interest in the aspects of presentation of values, adjustment of interest structure and change of communication strategy. We may make more friends if we recognize their shared values. It is only by actively pushing forward political system reform, actively taking part in multilateral affairs and global governance, strengthening strategic mutual trust and exploring cooperative areas, that we are able to push the international order to move in the direction of more fairness and more justice. Thus, we may avoid opposition and isolation which may be caused by failure in publicizing the common values of freedom, democracy, fairness, human rights, rule of law and justice.

"Top-down design" and overall promotion of political system reform is not only a built-in logic for the cause of China's socialist modernization construction, but also the essential requirement of the Chinese nation to realize the great renewal. Through exploration for over half a century, we have initially formed the socialist theories, systems and the road to move forward with Chinese characteristics. Presently, standing at such a milestone, in the era of globalization, we should know how to more actively fulfill the "top-down design" of the political system's reform, more rationally objectively and effectively maintain the state's benefits, and continuously improve our social and political systems, thus making our own contributions to human civilization and development, and make China's development road advance along with the historical progress of the whole world on the basis of surpassing the traditional socialist model and the development road of western countries. All these shall become very meaningful.

For the "top-down design" of political system reform, it is necessary, first, to realize new breakthroughs in ideology, and further realize new breakthroughs in reform. History and practice have proved: when there is a breakthrough, there is fast and healthy development. "Practice is the sole criterion for testing truth" and is a breakthrough of "the class struggle is the core" and the "two whatevers" philosophy. This breakthrough successfully realized the shift of the work focus of the Party and the state and started things in the right direction, thus to begin the great cause of reform and opening up; the idea that "planning and market are both economic means" rather than "the essential distinction between socialism and capitalism" broke the concept that confined us as to whether it was a socialist or capitalist approach, and thus energetically promoted the establishment of the system of a socialist market economy. For the time being, we are facing a critical period. Whether breakthroughs can be made with courage and wisdom in the reform of the political system and development of democracy will decide whether the great cause of socialism with Chinese characteristics may develop successfully and whether the Chinese nation can truly realize the great renewal.

For the "top-down design" of political system reform, it is necessary, second, to fully realize the political superstructure of socialism and "to be more adaptable to the development and change of the economic foundation." Marx used to point out explicitly, "People will develop a certain necessary relationship that is not to be transferred with their will in their social production, i.e. the production relationship that is adaptable to a certain development stage of their material productivity. The total of these production relationships constitute the economic structure of society, i.e. the realistic foundation on which the legal and political superstructure is built and which matches certain social ideological patterns. The production mode of material life constrains the whole process of social life, political life and spiritual life." The political superstructure, i.e. the political and legal systems and facilities and the political ideology must be adapted to the change of the economic foundation. China's construction of a socialist market economic system has achieved great success in the over 30 years of reform. The ownership relationship, distribution mode, and social interest structure have all undergone huge changes. These changes of the economic foundation will certainly require the improvement and development of the political superstructure to be adapted to it. To actively push forward the reform of the social and legal systems is both an important part of the overall reform and the objective requirement to guarantee the fruits of the economic system reform.

Third, the "top-down design" of political system reform will necessarily require us to put more focus on "overall planning and defining the priorities and key tasks of reform" on the basis of "crossing the river by feeling the stones," in order to have a clear understanding and overall planning and design of the goals, paths, stages, conditions, difficulties and the outlook of the reform. In the early days of reform and opening up, in general, we did not make deep enough conclusions and analysis of the historical experiences of our revolution and construction, and did not have a full understanding of the development status of other countries in the world. Therefore, we always held the principle of practice, continuously experimented and explored and admitted the bounded rationality. There is the historical necessity and reasonability for us to "cross the river by feeling the stones," and we have created great effects in practice. Nowadays, we have a certain economic foundation, much experience and many lessons, positive and/or negative, and talent accumulation and think tanks, and we have a clearer understanding than ever before about the development model of ourselves and other countries. Therefore, we are fully facilitated and capable of designing and planning the future reform and development in strategic thinking, and systematically defining the goals, direction, areas, focus, systems, mechanisms, etc. We can no longer go with the stream. In order to make a good overall design and planning, we must keep these ideas as guidelines: in terms of goal, "to follow people of all ethnic groups' with a new expectation of living a better life"; in terms of motivation, "by continuing to take reform as the strong motivation for speeding economic development, we must push forward the reforms of various areas with greater will and courage," in terms of focus and priorities, we must "energetically promote the economic system reform, push forward the political system reform actively and steadily, and accelerate the reform of cultural systems and social systems," in terms of subject, we must "further mobilize the activities of reform in all groups and respect the pioneering spirit of the masses."

Fourth, the "top-down design" of political system reform will objectively require us to follow the path of "incremental reform," and actively drive "democracy" and "rule of law" into practice from texts within the existing political and legal frameworks, so as to mobilize democracy. From the founding of the PRC to the reform and opening up, the Party and the state have constructed the most complete regulations on citizen rights protection in the constitution and legal documents; defining the clearest boundaries for government power; and developing a rational political system in which law-making, administration and judiciary support will check each other. In practice, however, the spirit of constitution has not been deeply implemented, citizens' rights are not fully protected, and the government's power is not efficiently constrained. The operation of the systems for the people's congress, the political consultative conference, government, judiciary and political party still retain the traces of the traditional politics: obvious officialdom, arbitrary policy making and a weak sense of following rules. For the overall promotion of political system reform, it is necessary for the people's congress to exert its role as the supreme power; to change the positioning of the political consultative conference that it is an honor conferred to the public, and break its mental state of being a "secondary institution" and "nursing institution," so as to include the political consultation into the process of decision-making; to ensure the judicial authority to exert power independently, and evade the interference from the administrative authority, social groups and individuals; and to make NGOs and common people play a constructive role between the state and the market. We will explore this wider space if we materialize legal documents and activate institutional texts in practice.

Finally, for the "top-down design" of political system reform, we should learn all the excellent fruits of human political civilizations with a more open mind and a broader vision. There is no precedent example of constructing democracy and rule of law in China, a country with a feudal political tradition lasting for thousands of years. In order to create the democracy that is more developed than a capitalist society, we have to seriously and systematically learn all the excellent fruits of human political civilizations. In the area of economy, we have learned some systems which used to be taken as exclusively capitalist, such as the corporate system and joint-stock system, and have learned to distribute resources by effectively utilizing the market. In the process of political system reform, we will not copy any specific model of the West. But democracy, rule of law, freedom, human rights, fairness and fraternity are not exclusive to the West. They are fruits of civilization to be shared by all human beings and are values to be pursued by all human beings. Socialism of course needs democracy and rule of law. There is no socialism and no socialist modernization without democracy.

Compared to the economic system reform, it is evident that the political system reform is lagging behind, and it is commonly agreed that it is necessary to begin the "top-down design" and actively push forward the political system reform. But in pushing forward the political system reform, it is more necessary to be alert on several wrong misunderstandings and stereotyped concepts. The first wrong misunderstanding is: the political system reform will bring turmoil and destroy stability, and then we will lose the good situation of economic development. In fact, the stability is only superficial and languid without political system reform, and it is necessary to push forward the political system reform for truly maintaining stability. We must monitor powers before we are able to eliminate conflicts effectively and realize the true stability. Conceptually, we must also break the tendency of "demonizing" democracy. The second wrong misunderstanding is that the political system should be accomplished in one stroke. Political system reform is a process. There are different goals for different stages. The top-down political system reform is not to fabricate an ultimate goal out of nothing. The third wrong misunderstanding is: consistency in policies is necessary since the political system reform is planned and designed in an overall way. The "top-down design" does not mean uniform treatment. The "top-down design" also needs grassroots experimental practices and exploration. To design the political system reform from top to down is also creating conditions for the grassroots reform to go deeper and free the grassroots reform from the embarrassment of "return to the original state in case nothing is done at the higher level," on the basis of respecting diversification and complex reality.

What kind of political system to implement and what kind of political development road to take for a country is determined by the specific situation of that country and the historical and cultural conditions, determined by the wisdom and courage of the ruling party and the public shown in dealing with complex problems, but ultimately, determined by the will of the overwhelming majority of the people of the country. We should always keep the Party's tradition of "maintaining close ties with the masses," be clear about the reality in which the masses "come to contact" us, and always be alert to the challenges that the masses no longer "come to contact" us in the future. For political system reform, we must hold the principle of seeking truth from facts, focusing on settling realistic problems rather than meaningless symbolism, with an objective, rational and tolerant attitude rather than through extreme and emotional appeal. It is only in this way that China's socialist political system reform may be promoted actively and steadily. The arduousness and complexity of the reform requires us to plan the strategy of reform on a high level, in order to make the reform leap from quantitative changes to qualitative changes. Being better prepared for unexpected development is more helpful to long-term ruling than being overly optimistic.

10

Dilemma and Breakthrough for China's Rule of Law:

Reflection on Several Issues About the Legal System Construction of China

Jiang Ping

Jiang Ping

Famous jurist, tenure professor of China University of Political Science and Law, doctoral supervisor of civil and commercial law, and expert with outstanding contributions and expert entitled to government subsidy as approved by the State Council. Served as member of the Seventh National People's Congress, member of the Standing Committee and deputy director of the Legal Committee of the Seventh National People's Congress; served as president of the China University of Political Science and Law and deputy chairman of the China Law Society; lectured on Chinese civil law, Roman law and company law at the Ghent University (Belgium), the University of Hong Kong, University of Rome Tor Vergata (Italy), Aoyama

Gakuin University (Japan), and Columbia University, and was honored with an Honorary Doctorate in Law by Ghent University (Belgium) and an Honorary Doctorate in Law by the Pontifical Catholic University of Peru. Currently serving as a distinguished advisor of the Supreme People's Court, arbitrator of the International Arbitration Commission, honorary director of the Beijing Arbitration Commission, and chairman of the China Society of Comparative Law.

Absence of Market Freedom, Market Order and Legal System Construction

It seems to me that freedom and order is an eternal theme of the legal system construction in China. Why do I say this? Because we know the goal of legal system construction is to solve the problems with freedom and order, either to a society or to a market.

Freedom is a drive for social development. Similarly, if there is no freedom for our market economy, it will lose the drive for advancement. I remember I got to know the Anti-Cartel Law (Anti-monopoly Law) of Germany during one visit to Germany. I felt so strange then: Marxism-Leninism had taught us a very important theory, that is, imperialism was monopolistic capitalism, but why did imperialism oppose monopoly instead of protecting it? I asked my German companions. They replied that the reason was simple: the core drive for the Western market economy is free competition, without which there will be no drive for advancement, so we oppose any practice that goes against free competition, either state monopoly or private monopoly. The law we promote as the most important is freedom in competition, which is one of the most fundamental principles.

Order is about security. If there is no personal security and no market security in the society where we live, then there is no opportunity to achieve the basic goal of legal system construction. So I think that legal system construction for a market economy encompasses two "securities": one is security of freedom, and the other is security of order. These represent two very important principles.

Based on the status quo in China, we should admit that we are deficient in market freedom and market order construction. This is somewhat different from western countries. The economy market construction of western countries, based on the economic liberalism proposed by Adam Smith, underwent a process of mature free competition. So when the economic crisis arrived in later years, people found that they had been over free. So then there emerged Keynesianism, an approach with which the state controls the market. But the market economy of China was transitioning from a planned economy which originally lacked freedom, so it is fair to say that our market was faced with double deficiencies in the very beginning: first, we were deficient in the market freedom which was developed and mature in the West, or what we had presented more was the upstart freedom out of the primary accumulation; second, our market was not completely opened and many transactions were under stringent control by the state. Some Chinese were complacent when the economic crisis occurred in America, believing that we avoided the financial crisis because we were so lucky that we did not do transactions of financial derivatives. In fact, when measured with the standard for a mature market economy, our market economy is underdeveloped. Futures, share options, and stock index futures which have just been started, for instance, are market transactions under stringent control by the state. Therefore, some say that China's market economy is perhaps a market economy in the era of electric bicycles, or a market economy that has entered in the era of autos, meaning we have not entered a relatively developed market economy. In this sense, there is great deficiency in guaranteeing market freedom.

But in comparison, what we lack in constructing market order is even more. It is fair to say China adopted the law-making for market freedom for quite a long time, but China neglected the law-making for market order in a certain way. We have not done enough in making laws concerning market order, including Contract Law, Company Law, Negotiable Instrument Law and Maritime Law. The absence of market order is typically reflected in the absence of credibility. Recently, many media reported the scandals of 18 Chinese companies listed in the US being suspended or delisted. In 2011, financial scandals of the Chinese companies listed in the US were exposed one after another, dragging the shares of China's concept stock into a drastic plunge. Within the two months from March to May 2011, 18 Chinese companies were suspended by NASDAQ or the New York Stock Exchange, and 4 companies were compelled to be delisted. This showed that the dishonesty and incredibility of certain Chinese enterprises had created a severe situation. I remember, when people talked about an enterprise going public, "packaging" was a favored term. The so-called packaging for going public meant the loss of the enterprise was changed into a profit in the books, which was obviously a fraud. Some companies listed in America even tried harder in packaging for going public, which made the American accounting firms feel embarrassed: there would be no market if the listing of Chinese companies were not approved, but they had to take on the risk of breaching business ethnics if they wanted to keep their market shares. So this was a severe problem. It is fair to say that the manipulation of accounts is very common in the enterprises of China. It was no wonder that former Premier Mr. Zhu Rongji defined the motto for the National Accounting Institute as "no manipulation of accounts," which was a great surprise to all. A university motto as explicit as "no manipulation of accounts" is an accurate reminder of some of the severest problems in this aspect in China.

The incredibility of enterprises is also reflected in some other aspects, such as the prevalent fake goods and fraudulent conduct, which are commonly seen in the market of China. China is ranked top in terms of speed of economic development, but lagging far behind in terms of market order. The disorder of China's market economy used to make China very embarrassed, including the cases in which 18 Chinese companies listed in America were suspended or delisted, which made Chinese commodities suffer a great loss of credibility in the world. Things are better now, but such problems are still severe and have to be solved as soon as possible.

In this sense, the goals for our legal system construction are: first, adequate freedom to the market; second, maintain stable order for the market. If we do not achieve these two goals, it means our legal system construction is still far away from our expectations.

Undoubtedly, freedom and order are the two sides of a conflict. If we overstress freedom and neglect order, there will be no stable security; conversely, if we overstress order and neglect freedom, the situation will still be the one without order and freedom. Of freedom and order, we should say that freedom is primarily guaranteed by private law.

We know that there are public law and private law. Some think the boundary between public law and private law has been weakened, but the basic demarcation is still there. Private law is about autonomy. In the area of private law, it is for the client to decide how to execute his or her rights. Market order is involved in the scope of public law, which includes administration and enforcement. For example, the new draft of the Trust Law of China includes the provisions of private law and public law. That is to say, the draft of the Trust Law includes not only the rights and obligations of every aspect of trust and the position of the trusted property, but also such issues as how to establish a trust company, how to administer the trust industry and how to evade trust risks, and so on. But it was found in the process of formulation that it was easier to formulate the Trust Law in terms of private law, but it was more complicated to deal with public law which involves administration of the trust industry. So the Japanese experts who helped us formulate the Trust Law believed that the private law and public law in the Trust Law should be formulated separately. We had to accept the advice of the Japanese experts. Finally, in drafting the Trust Law, we were unable to finish the public law for the Trust Law, so we promulgated the Trust Law only with private law. But problems arose. Recently, at a seminar of the trust industry, everyone all agreed that it was inadequate only to have private law. Although there were some orders and regulations issued by the State Council, it was impossible to guarantee the security of the trust industry without public law. So in this point, it is very important to make laws in a systematic way. We made the Trust Law, but we do not have the Law of Trust Industry and no Tax Law. How shall trust companies pay tax? What are the conditions for trust company establishment? But there are neither relevant regulations nor state requirements. How could the security deposit be kept safe in the process of operation? We have none of these guidelines.

Normally, a country has to go through three stages from overstressing market freedom to equal consideration of both market freedom and order. In the earliest stage, it was primarily to guarantee the freedom in the market through the Civil Law, but the issue of market order was also mentioned. Take the relationship between sale and purchase. There were frauds in the past, but the principle for dealing with such things was for the buyer to be more careful so as not to be cheated by the seller. If you were cheated, it was because you did not understand very well the principle of purchase and sale. But people came to find that such principles were wrong: it was not enough for the buyer to be careful, but it was necessary to find out the fraudulent conduct of the seller. Hence some measures against fraud have been formulated. There are such key provisions in the Civil Code of Germany. Similarly, honesty and credibility are key provisions in the Company Law: the parties to the contract, once the contract is signed, have to follow the principles of honesty and credibility in the first place. How could things work out without honesty and credibility? These issues can be dealt with basically by following the civil regulations.

In the second stage, it is to solve the new problems involved in the Commercial Law. Let's take the most typical Securities Law as an instance. The Securities Law is the most important law for settling commercial cases. But in China, the Securities Law is included in the Commercial Law, while in Taiwan it is included in administrative regulations. This is within public law, because in the Securities Law, it is not only to guarantee the freedom of both parties of a securities transaction, but also to deal with fraudulent conduct in the process of transactions and to prevent such frauds. We adopted this approach in later commercial laws.

In the last stage, the system of economic laws emerges. America, for example, adopted the Sherman Act in 1890. This act was famous for anti-monopoly. In the past, mergers were only the business between two enterprises, but it was not that way after the Act was passed. If two big enterprises merged, the merger would do harm to others, because it occupied too many market shares and pushed others out of market. So with regard to this, there should be some special regulations in the legal system. That's why all these laws, including Anti-monopoly Law, Anti Unfair Competition Law, Anti-dumping Law, and Statute of Frauds, etc., were promulgated as economic laws.

Although there is no absolute demarcation between the three stages, we may still find some built-in connections between them. It means that the law puts more and more stress on the protection of market order. This explains the development process that, in the beginning, the protection of order was taken as a minor part in the Civil Law, then taken as a very important part in the commercial law, and finally taken as the core in the economic law; the Anti-monopoly Law is even seen as the constitution for the economic area.

Be on the Alert that State Power Could over Interfere with Market

It is not a fresh topic of state power interfering with a market in today's world. State power, either of socialist countries or western countries, is employed to interfere with the market. I think this is a very important policy we adopt now for the market.

To establish the socialist market economy is the greatest common divisor, and this is the goal accepted by the Left and the Right, conservative or liberal, in the world of economics. But the opinions are divided as to how to understand the socialist market economy. Years ago, a large enterprise from Hong Kong established a prize in the Mainland, in order to award the older generation of economists who made contributions to the economic development of China. There were four recipients, two of which are still alive, i.e. Liu Guoguang and Wu Jinglian. Professor Wu Jinglian used to say to me, the focuses of the speeches made by the two of them were different when the award was conferred in the Great Hall of the People. Liu Guoguang believed that, since we spoke of a socialist market economy, the characteristics should be state control, which was weakened in the past because we did not follow the correct guidelines of a market economy. But Wu Jinglian thought on the contrary. He put the focus on the market economy, believing that the state interfered too much. The disagreement between the two scholars is very representative, and such disagreement also makes us think about these issues: How big is the role the state is playing in dealing with the relationship between state and market? And how large is the scope in which the role is played? This should be a very important issue worth discussion.

With regard to market freedom, the focus is put on market access and resource distribution. The state should not interfere too much in these aspects, i.e. market access and resource distribution. A story, with a very marked title, "Zhejiang's State-owned Capital Entering almost Every Area of the Agricultural Product Market," was published in *Legal Daily* on June 23 of this year. I was astonished at this story, for there have been very few such stories in many years. The tradition of Zhejiang tells us that the private economy is developed, but now it was the state-owned capital that is going to enter the agricultural product market. The reason is that the agricultural product market is in disorder. With too big a percentage of private enterprises in the market, there are many frauds and false and fake products, and even some toxic products, so the government believes the system does not work very successfully and the property ownership is too complicated. In the early days of reform and opening up, however, what we emphasized was to give bigger freedom to private enterprises in agricultural markets and small commodity markets. Why is it now changed to the situation that the state-owned capital is going to have an overall control over the market? So I was worried whether it was a sign of a return to the planned economy. We may feel the situation is worse from the power shortages of many provinces in the south this year, for instance. In many places, some enterprises stopped work for one day every three days, and even some stopped for two days each week. How should we solve the problem of power shortages? There was a story in the newspapers that the National Development and Reform Commission (NDRC) sped up the approval for establishing power stations in order to solve the power shortage problem. I was deeply impressed by this. The NDRC sped up the approval only when the power shortage grew very serious, but when the approved projects were completed, the power supply would be in a surplus situation. Some problems occurring in the planned economy are repeated even more often in this era of the market economy. It is not following the law of the market economy to solve power shortages completely through approval of new power stations. We often say that the construction of a power station must go through the steps from a number of divisions and bureaus under the NDRC. The construction of a power station for solving power shortages cannot be decided by the province itself, but has to be approved by a division under the NDRC, and it would not be carried out without this approval. In the planned economy, the consequences caused by the approval of some projects by cadres at division-level were obviously severe. So in this sense, our market freedom is faced with a greater regression now, because the state strengthens and restores some approval procedures.

The fact is the state had a good wish in promulgating the Administrative Licensing Law. It was hoped that the problems that could be solved through the market economy should be solved by the market itself, those that could not be solved should be solved by NGOs as much as possible, and only those that could not be solved either by the market or NGOs were to be reviewed and approved by the state. So in the three priorities, the state review and approval is put in the third position, meaning that state power is to be employed only after the problems are found too difficult to be solved by the market and society. For the time being, however, the power of state approval has become increasingly bigger. After the global economic crisis, relevant government authorities passed a number of approval documents requiring that key industries and sectors, including shipbuilding and steel industries, etc., be brought under administrative control. Anyone that fails to reach the standard shall be weeded out or reorganized. This approach strengthened the government control in a disguised way. The negative effects produced by this approach are worth our reflection.

We will also approach this problem by observing market order. There was an important law regulating market order, Product Quality Law, made by the Seventh National People's Congress. During the process of making the law, discussions were carried out about what kind of measures the state should take to control product quality. We consulted the Product Liability Law of the US, whose purpose was similar to our Product Quality Law, that is, with guaranteeing product quality as the goal, but the measures taken were the opposite: in the American law, it was product liability that was used to promote product quality, meaning that you might be licensed to produce everything except drugs and food which might affect people's life and health. If the user was harmed by the fake products produced by you, you had to undertake the civil liabilities once the user raised a claim. In the Product

Quality Law made by us, administrative measures, rather than civil procedure, were primarily taken to strengthen management.

There is the issue of intellectual property. When I gave lectures in America in 1995, an American lawyer asked why the intellectual properties of America were infringed so much in China. I replied then, the law of intellectual property was developed later in China than America and Britain, and China has yet to establish a complete law enforcement system in the central government and local governments. Unexpectedly, the American lawyer refuted immediately: based on your thinking, how large a government was China going to build? I realized I was fooled at this question: if a separate law enforcement authority was established in the central government and local governments after each law was adopted in China, it was certain that the government would grow into a huge monster. Therefore, to us, it is an interesting question of how to improve the approach to law making.

China's Construction of Rule of Law Should Keep Up to Date

Rule of law or rule by man is the most fundamental issue China is faced with. In my view, China's rule of law is faced with a regression. In the past, I often said that China's rule of law was somewhat improved; but in general, it was advancing two steps and falling back one step, which was advancing anyway. But I may point out that it is falling back two steps and advancing one step in recent years. Regression has become the main action. This is horrible. If this situation lasts for a long time, our rule of law will be put in great danger.

I think we are perhaps concerned with the Li Zhuang Case. On December 12, 2009, Li Zhuang, a lawyer and partner of the Beijing Kangda Law Firm, was arrested by the Chongqing Public Security Bureau for being suspected of perjury when performing as attorney for Gong Gangmo, an alleged mafia boss in Chongqing. On February 9, 2010, the First Intermediate People's Court of Chongqing sentenced Li Zhuang to 18 months' imprisonment for the crime of giving false evidence and impairing testimony. On April 2, 2010, the People's Procuratorate of Jiangbei District, Chongqing, initiated a public prosecution of Li Zhuang to the People's Court of Jiangbei District, Chongqing, for the alleged crime of impairing testimony as defender. On April 28, 2011, the People's Court of Jiangbei District, Chongqing decided not to sue Li Zhuang and announced the decision to Li Zhuang. I am often asked about this case in different meetings. I am concerned with the Li Zhuang Case not for Li Zhuang the individual. I am no acquaintance to Li Zhuang and have no personal feelings for him. But I believe it is necessary to express my viewpoint for the sake of honoring the responsibilities of a lawyer.

The Li Zhuang Case is a regression of the rule by man, which was fully reflected in the "crime leak" added later. Li Zhuang was found guilty because he was accused of perjury, but in fact it is hard to discern and confirm perjury. What is perjury? If the perjury is written, like a fake ID card or a fake official document, it is obvious. But how could you define perjury in a testimony? In the first trial of Li Zhuang as defender, the testimony given by the defendant Gong Gangmo in the public security bureau was obtained by torturing him. Later he said that Li Zhuang incited him to withdraw the confession. It was in the doubt here. The police were present when Li Zhuang met Gong Gangmo. It is hard to explain how Li made Gong withdraw his confession in the presence of the police. One year after, the People's Procuratorate of Jiangbei District, Chongqing initiated a public prosecution of Li Zhuang to the People's Court of Jiangbei District, Chongqing, for the alleged crime of impairing testimony as defender. The cause of the case was that, after the sentence of the Li Zhuang Case was announced, the judicial authority of Chongqing received reports and it was going to look into the crime Li Zhuang committed in other criminal cases when he acted as attorney. Someone heard Li Zhuang was arrested and reported that Li Zhuang had also incited him to withdraw the confession. This person was sentenced for drug addiction and his mental status was not stable. It was not clear what the purpose of the reporter was, money borrowing or investment? Therefore, the People's Procuratorate finally withdrew the lawsuit. This withdrawal was completely correct. There were some legal reasons, because there was no accurate evidence. If someone reported that Li Zhuang incited him to withdraw the confession, it was very necessary for the person to be summoned to court for testimony at least. But the witness was not called to give testimony, and the letter of accusation was taken as the only evidence, which was very ridiculous.

The Li Zhuang Case is a typical reflection of a very important problem with the judicial system of China for the present, that is, the judicial system fails to play the role of protecting attorneys. This does not mean that it is impossible to sentence lawyers, but means that special consideration should be made on sentencing lawyers. If a lawyer commits perjury and there is a written one, it can be explained well. But if it is an oral testimony, then the witness must be interrogated at court, and the cross-examination by both prosecutor and defender should be allowed. This cross-examination is very important, because the questions raised by both prosecutor and defender may expose what the witness testifies to be either true or false. How could there be democracy to be spoken of if our lawyers are often brought under such circumstances? How could things work out if a lawyer feels the risk of taking on criminal liabilities in defending?

People asked me several times, was it the legal reason or political reason for the withdrawal of the crime leak of Li Zhuang? I said it was not very clear. But I personally think that the withdrawal of the crime leak of Li Zhuang is both a legal victory and a victory for support of public opinions. There was a big legal loophole, and the Procuratorate would lose support in terms of legality if it decided to continue their way. Was there any political reason? I think there was. Many were made to feel that "he who has a mind to beat his dog will easily find his stick" when the prosecution of Li Zhuang for a crime leak was raised again.

Is it not easy to add another crime to a person who is already sentenced? So, the second prosecution of Li Zhuang for a crime leak lost the support of the public and the legal world.

Why should someone hang on an ordinary lawyer and set him in the deathtrap? This is not the right way. I think the statesmen of China should think about this issue.

To Understand the Relationship Between "Two Beliefs" and the Legal System Construction

There are two popular catchwords, which are most easily to be twisted among grassroots officials today. One is the belief of "maintaining stability is of top priority," and the other is the belief of "uniqueness of China's situation." These are the "two beliefs" I have mentioned. I think we should pay attention to its negative impact on the legal system construction under the conditions of China. The proposal of the "two beliefs" has its reasonability, but it is also easy to be misused and twisted in practice. According to the belief of "maintaining stability is of top priority," how could the reform be carried out without stability? How could there be development without this? So it is somewhat justified to take stability as the priority. Seeing the belief of "uniqueness of China's situation," I would say the situation of every country is unique. Every country has its unique situation. But these two beliefs must be proposed in a specific atmosphere and for a specific purpose, and they have great impact on the legal system construction and governance by law of China. We should have a correct understanding of the relationship between the two.

It is interesting to note that it is hard for us to define what stability is in practice. We do not have the "method of stability," and it is not clear to us how to define the cases of destroying stability. It is all for the top leaders of the Party committee and the government to define whether this is stable or not. When we propose "maintaining stability is of top priority," it follows a realistic question: who shall define whether it is stable or not? Or, who shall define whether something affects stability? There is no law or any other clear demarcation to define who shall define whether something affects stability. It is fair to say that whether something is stable or not is completely defined by the local Party and government top leaders. Currently, it is not only the mayor, but also the secretary of the Party committee of a county government and county magistrate that may decide whether some behavior affects stability in their place. Therefore, it is possible to cause the principle of "rule by man" to propose "maintaining stability is of top priority" in a generalized way.

Let's look at Shenzhen, a forerunner of reform and opening up. It is going to host the World University Games in the near future. In order to maintain the security for the Games, the municipal government of Shenzhen promulgated a measure, in order to have strict monitoring over those who might be highly dangerous to social security, and defined 80,000 people into 7 categories as dangerous to society according to their way of categorizing. The municipal government of Shenzhen disapproved their residence in Shenzhen and ordered them to move away. Where did the Shenzhen government drive the 80,000 people? It was certain that the 80,000 people were reluctant to return to their hometown, so they had no other choice but move to nearby cities. Then, how could the security of those nearby cities be maintained? As expected, the governments of the nearby cities, including Dongguan and Huizhou responded radically by copying the measure of Shenzhen. The reason held by them was that if these people came to Dongguan and Huizhou, who was to take care of our security? China would be put in great danger if such logic was followed.

Shenzhen took a bad lead. There were loud different public voices after the measure was promulgated. This measure by the Shenzhen government essentially violated the fundamental principle of the Constitution. It is stipulated in the Constitution that everyone is equal and no one should be discriminated due to their registered household. But what is the situation now? An exaggerated conclusion could be that it is similar to the policy on the people of lower social status in India, or the policy of Capitis deminutio (personality reduction/derogation) in ancient Rome, that is, to divide people into different social levels rather than treat everyone as equal citizens. This is an essential problem that affects the guarantee of our human rights.

But I found in a news story that, regardless of the opposite voice, the deputy mayor of Shenzhen, who also acted as director of the public security bureau decided that the measure should be carried out. The reason given by the Shenzhen government was that "maintaining stability is of top priority," and these 80,000 people must leave Shenzhen because they were believed to affect stability. But how could the officials of Shenzhen define whether these people would affect stability or not? The reason primarily given was that the rule by man played a major role. We should reflect: if we defined whether something was stable or not through rule by man, or even the top leader of a local government or a director of a public security bureau, was China going in the direction of rule by man again? Was China going to regress to the rule by man? This would be horrible. But the problem is that worse things are yet to come. For China, the place which is expected to carry forward the spirit of reform and opening up should implement a backward measure. How could we check them? Could we check them through the constitutional approach? It is difficult. There are no constitutional proceedings in China, so it is impossible for us to file a lawsuit against this. What we could do is at most copy the manner with which the three doctors petitioned to the Standing Committee for the Sun Zhigang Case. If the State Council is wise enough, it could cancel the regulation about sheltering for investigation; but what if the government was not wise? There is no relief measure to stop this practice. Therefore, from this perspective, we should indeed need to solve a series of problems, including constitutional proceedings.

There was another story in the newspapers. A local court made a judgment about a case, but the judgment was resisted by the local government in enforcement. The local government required the court to stop the enforcement with the reason that such judgment would affect "stability." The court believed the judgment was made by law and the judgment had taken effect. But some leader in the county government remarked that there were many citizens who were against this and the government disapproved the enforcement. The local government interfered with the court enforcement for the reason that those people objected to it. Is not this a case in which "stability" is placed superior to rule of law? In the name of "maintaining stability is of top priority," the administrative power openly interfered with the administration of justice, which is not rare in the grassroots administration. The enforcement of a judgment by law is a reflection of governance by law, but how could China become a state ruled by law if a judgment cannot be enforced in cases like this? Stability should be based on rule of law.

Then let's see the belief of "uniqueness of China's situation." China's situation is of course unique, but is there any country and region whose situation is not unique? Even the situation of the Macao Special Administrative Region is unique in that, for example, Macao has its own laws, which is not the same with other places in the world. The situation of the Hong Kong Special Administrative Region is also unique, but it is also a society ruled by law. So we should be clear that there are three levels of law we speak of: law is a system, an approach, and more a philosophy.

As a system, law varies across countries. The legal system of China absolutely has some regulations characteristic of China, such as its land policies. Is there the land contracted responsibility system in other countries? Is there the land collective ownership in other countries? There is not. Therefore, in terms of specific systems, China has her uniqueness. But as an approach, laws share something in common. In terms of approach, it is clear that we should collect evidence, take facts as the basis, and judge how the evidence is in analyzing a legal issue. Americans are interested in approaches. When you study law in the US and you ask your teacher "what is your opinion" after a lecture is over, the teacher would tell you "I've no opinion; what I taught is only the approach." The reason is that approach is the deep basis for the system. The legal system will change anytime with the changes of eras, while the approach is more stable. In a sense, it is more important to learn an approach than a system.

Do not forget that there is a common philosophy in rule of law. It is the common goal for each country since the beginning of development. We may say that China is special and different from other countries in the world. But the laws we adopt today is an order. Law serves as rules for social life and serves as rules for market economy, so rules shares something in common. I think freedom, democracy, human rights, and fairness and justice are the goals pursued by human beings. A law will lose its name if it fails to maintain fairness and justice. A law will lose its name if we are not entitled to freedom and human rights. So in this sense, we have to find a lot in common in laws. These common qualities cannot be covered by individual features, and at the same time cannot be covered by a country by stressing its national characteristics. Therefore, in this sense, the law, as a philosophy, cannot do without freedom, democracy, human rights, and fairness and justice. As remarked by Premier Wen Jiabao in his speech delivered at The Royal Society of the UK, the future China is going to be a country that fully realizes democracy, rule of law, fairness and justice. The philosophy that China in the future will fully realize democracy, rule of law, fairness and justice has shown our direction of progress. So it is without doubt that governance by law should be put on the agenda.

11

Where Is the Road to Anti-Corruption for China[1]

He Zengke

He Zengke

Director and Research Fellow of the World Strategy Development Research Department, Central Compilation & Translation Bureau, Deputy Director of the China Government Innovation Center of Peking University, Party-time Researcher of the Clean Government Research Office of Tsinghua University, Director of the China Association of Political Science, Chief Expert of the subproject of the Project of Marxist Basic Theory Research and Construction as initiated by the CPC Central Committee. His major research area is contemporary China's politics, and the research focuses on corruption and anti-corruption, civil society and the Third Sector, local governance and government innovation, social construction and social management, etc.

---

[1] Originally published in *China Reform*, 2011(4).

for the next stage through...improving the vertical accountability system in the citizen's right for election and the horizontal system of checks and balances."

—He Zengke

opening up, proposing to establish a system of punishing and preventing corruption inclusive of education, supervision, and system construction, i.e. a national anti-corruption system with Chinese characteristics. These efforts have achieved some effect, which is, however, quite limited on the whole. This is closely related to the fact that the present anti-corruption system is characteristic of a traditional centralized political system and that the lagging behind of the political system reform has further restricted the exertion of its functions.

It is essential for China to carry out anti-corruption and power supervision for the next stage through deepening the reform of the political system, realizing the modern transition in the national anti-corruption system, and improving the vertical accountability system in the citizen's right for election and the horizontal system of checks and balances.

Severe Anti-Corruption Situation

Since 1949, China has primarily established a system of punishing and preventing anti-corruption, from mass movement, to system construction, then to the construction of a punishment and prevention system, that is, a national anti-corruption system with Chinese characteristics. This system includes:

(1) Having established the goal system of building a clean ruling party and a clean government, i.e. scientific development, with a harmonious and overall well-off society;

(2) Having set various institutional supports for the national anti-corruption system: the leading system and working mechanism for anti-corruption inclusive of the centralized leadership of the CPC committee, cooperative management of the Party and the government, organization and coordination of the discipline inspection committee, respective duties of each department, support and participation from the public;

(3) Having improved some core rules essential to normal functioning of some institutional supports, such as improving the rules on the inner-party

(4) Having made the value system of clean government, accepted by the public and civil servants, through fostering a culture of clean government and education in a clean government.

However, the institutional supports for the anti-corruption system did not develop in a balanced way. Only a few institutional supports have played their duel role, including the Party committee, government, and special supervision authority, but the other institutional supports have exerted very limited functions, clearly a "short slab." The core rules for these institutional supports are unreasonably absent, and the vertical accountability mechanism for election and the horizontal accountability mechanism of checks and balances are incomplete, which prevents power supervision and restraint from forming a closed circle. All these problems have a serious negative impact on the functioning of the national anti-corruption system, whose ineffectiveness leads to a limited effect on anti-corruption.

Presently, there are still some typical corruptions in China: the first is the corruptions committed by the major leaders or top leaders of Party Committees and governments at different levels, which occur one after another and become almost incurable; the second is the evil corruptions in terms of personnel arrangements and judiciaries are becoming more and more serious; the third is the malpractices and the style of extravagances and waste which cannot be terminated; the fourth is the tendency of the legalization of the privileges enjoyed by some civil servants, especially the cadres, in housing, medical treatment, car use and welfare; the fifth is the unbalanced and inconsistent punishment of the corrupt ones and low-possibilities of discovery and disposal; the sixth is punishment based on Party and government disciplines rather than laws and the tendency in which the punishment and penalties are based on Party and government disciplines that replace the punishment of law.

The modern national anti-corruption system is a collective name referring to a series of institutions and rules reflecting the vertical accountability mechanism for citizen election and the horizontal principle of checks and balances. In terms of supervising and restraining power and preventing and punishing corruption, the effectiveness standards include the comprehensive effectiveness standard and the branch-specific effectiveness standard.

The overall effectiveness standard for the national anti-corruption system refers to three aspects: all the institutional supports are developed in a balanced way that they rely on each other and restrain each other; the core rules essential to institutional supports are universally established for them to fully perform their duties and functions; power supervision and restraint are presented in a closed circle, with the vertical and horizontal accountability mechanisms with the election system and the principle of checks and balances as the core are implemented throughout the institutions and rule systems, meaning there should be no public power and civil servants who are not brought under supervision and restraint. The effectiveness of institutions and rules included in each anti-corruption support may be also evaluated with different standards (see Table 1).

Table 1   Standards for evaluating the effectiveness of the national anti-corruption system

Overall effectiveness standard	Institutional effectiveness	Rule effectiveness
Balanced development of institutional supports	Independence	Completeness
	Coordination	Authoritativeness
Universal establishment of core rules	Professionalism	Operability
	Matching	Desirability
Power supervision and restraint in a closed circle	Appropriateness	Sustainability
	Transparency	Multi-win
	Accountability degree	Compatibility

Source: Prepared by the author based on relevant theories of Transparency International.

According to Table 1, the standards for evaluating the effectiveness of the national anti-corruption system, which can be found in China, and the anti-corruption system to fully play their roles, are still notably absent or incomplete, which further affects the exertion of the functions of the anti-corruption system (see Table 2).

Table 2 Assessment of overall status of China's national anti-corruption system presently

Institutional supports	Institutional availability (Yes/No)	Core rules	Rule availability (Yes/No)
All-level CPC committees as the core of leadership	Yes	Election accountability	No
All-level People's Congresses and their Standing Committees as the legislative body	Yes	Rules on guaranteeing the exercise of the veto power	
Non-Communist parties and Political Consultative Conference as the political supervisory body	Yes	Rules on responsibility-exemption for taking part in significant decision-making and opinions	
Government administrative body	Yes	Rules on dealing with conflicts between public and private interests	Partly
Auditory body	Yes	Independence	No
Authority of discipline inspection and monitor as the body monitoring the administrative power	Yes	Rules on guaranteeing the independence from the subject for supervision	No
Procuratorate and the bureau of corruption prevention as the special anti-corruption body	Yes	Enforceable and strictly enforced anti-corruption laws	Partly
Court as the judicial system	Yes	Independence	Partly
System of civil servants	Yes	Moral standards on public services relating to cadres' personnel system	Partly
Local governments in the vertical-horizontal relations	Yes	Rules reflecting subsidiarity	No
Public sectors	Yes	Governance structure with transparency, participation and accountability	Partly
Sectors of private economy	Yes	Policies encouraging competition	Partly
Media, including network media	Yes	Free expression	Partly
Civil society	Yes	Rules on guaranteeing the right of speech	Partly
International community	Yes	Effective and mutual legal or judicial coordination	Partly

Source: Prepared by the author based on relevant data.

national institutional supports, which are all established by the core rules for guaranteeing the institutional supports for the national anti-corruption system to fully play their roles, are absent or incomplete. The 15 institutional supports are developed in an unbalanced way.

Based on the seven evaluation standards as defined above, as well as the reality of the functional construction of each institutional support, the effectiveness of these standards can be evaluated. Let's put them into three scales, i.e. 3, 2, and 1 representing the high, medium and low degree of how each evaluation standard is met respectively (see Table 3).

According to Table 3, in the supervision and accountability system as constructed by the 15 institutional supports, the top-down supervision accountability practiced by Party Committees at all levels is the most effective, except the force from the international community linked through conventions; the second most effective is the top-down administrative accountability practiced by all-level governments; the third most effective is the party discipline and government discipline supervision practiced by the body of discipline inspection and monitor; the fourth most effective is the supervision carried out by special supervision authorities, including auditory institutions, procuratorates, and courts. The supervision by the People's Congress is more effective than that of the non-Communist parties and the Political Consultative Conference. The supports from the social supervision accountability, other than the political power, include enterprises' supervision, netizens' supervision, media supervision and civil supervision, from most effective to least effective.

It is necessary to point out that the unsatisfactory independence of the special supervision authorities, including the discipline inspection and monitoring authorities, auditory authorities, procuratorates and courts, affects the effective performance of their anti-corruption functions.

We are going to make a preliminary evaluation of the overall effectiveness of the construction of the anti-corruption rule system presently (see Table 4).

Name of institution/ effectiveness evaluation standard	Independence	Coordination	Professionalism	Matching	Appropriateness	Transparency	Accountability	Total
All-level CPC Committees as the core of leadership	3	3	1	3	3	1	1	15
All-level People's Congresses and their Standing Committees as the legislative body	1	2	2	1	2	2	1	11
Non-Communist parties and Political Consultative Conference as the political Supervisory body	1	1	3	1	1	1	1	9
Government administrative body	1	3	2	3	1	2	2	14
Auditory body	1	2	3	1	1	2	2	12
Authority of discipline inspection and monitor as the body monitoring the administrative power	1	3	3	3	2	1	1	13
Procuratorate and the bureau of corruption prevention as the special anti-corruption body	1	2	3	2	2	2	2	12
Court as the judicial system	1	2	3	2	1	2	1	12
System of civil servants	1	1	2	2	1	2	2	11
Local governments in the vertical-horizontal relations	1	1	2	1	1	2	1	9
Public sectors	2	1	2	2	1	2	1	11
Sectors of private economy	3	1	2	2	2	1	1	12
Media, incl. network media	1	1	2	1	1	2	1	9
Civil society	1	2	1	1	1	1	1	8
International community	3	1	3	1	1	3	2	14

Source: Prepared by the author based on relevant data.

Table 4　Effectiveness assessment of China's current anti-corruption rule system

Effectiveness standard	Completeness	Authoritativeness	Operability	Desirability	Sustainability	Multi-win	Compatibility
Rule system	Medium	Low	Low	Low	Low	Medium	

Source: Prepared by the author based on relevant data.

Table 4 shows that China's current anti-corruption system is at the medium level of completeness, but the anti-corruption rule system features unfavorable authoritativeness, operability, desirability, sustainability, multi-win and compatibility, so the overall quality of the anti-corruption rule system is not high.

The current national anti-corruption system in China features both some qualities of a modern national anti-corruption system and the clean government of the traditional centralized politics system. It is transitional and composite. Some central and difficult issues in the political system reform have been seriously lagging behind for a long time, so there are some insurmountable institutional and mechanism obstacles in supervising and restraining power and preventing and punishing corruptions in the existing national anti-corruption system, making the system less effective.

The first is immoderate centralization of power, making it difficult to implement effective supervision and restraint of the major leaders of the Party committee and governments at each level.

As early as 1957, Deng Xiaoping made a thorough analysis of the immoderate centralization of power. In 1980, Deng Xiaoping launched the reform of the leading system of the Party and the state. In 1987, the Thirteenth National Congress of the CPC raised a specific proposal on the separation between the Party and the government. However, separation between the Party and the government was faced with great obstacles and problems in practice, and relevant reform was suspended. The heads of the local Party committees and governments at different levels control the personnel arrangement and budgets, and it was difficult for the deputies to supervise them. The People's Congress and the People's Political Consultative Conference should be led by the leaders of the Party Committee at the same level on the one hand, and on the other, should listen to the government at the same level on such issues as personnel and budgets, so it is difficult for them to implement effective supervision. The accountability system in which the top leader should take the general accountabilities has made it easier for the top leaders of various authorities at various levels to gather all types of power in their own hands. Thus, the supervision over the top leaders has become a great difficulty, making them more and more corrupt.

The second is the management system in which the special supervision the supervisory effects and functions of the supervision authority.

Local special supervision authorities of discipline inspection and monitoring, audit and procuratorial working at all levels in China, all implemented the dual leadership system. The members of the discipline inspection and monitoring authority, as the special supervision body within the Party, are elected by the Congress of Party Representatives, but they are subject to the leadership of the same-level Party Committee that is also elected by the Congress of Party Representatives and should have been supervised by the discipline inspection and monitoring authority. The discipline inspection and monitoring authority is not independent from the same-level Party Committee in personnel arrangement, and the upper-level discipline inspection and monitoring authority only leads them in terms of professional guidance, so it is difficult for the discipline inspection and monitoring authority to supervise the same-level Party Committee, especially the top leaders.

As the special authorities that take charge of monitoring and audit of administrative authorities and their top leaders, the administrative monitoring authority and the auditory authority should have been subordinate to the People's Congress, but they are in fact subordinate to the administrative authority and report to the same-level administrative top leaders. The professional guidance from the upper-level discipline inspection and monitoring authority does not change the disadvantage that the administrative authority supervises itself.

The procuratorate, as the legal supervision authority, is subject to the leadership of both the same-level People's Congress and the same-level Party Committee, and their personnel and budget issues are controlled by the same-level local government. The professional guidance and personnel recognition power do not solve the problem of inadequate independence of the procuratorate.

The current management system of the special supervision authorities make the supervisor subordinate to the subject of supervision, lacking reasonable independence and authoritativeness, which result in the problems supervise, the same-level leaders of the Party and the government.

Third, the combination of legislative and executive powers makes it impossible to have a mechanism of checks and balances in which the decision-making power, the enforcement power and the oversight power are both separate from and restrained by each other.

It is the combination of legislative and executive powers that is practiced by all-level Party Committees and People's Congresses in China, the decision-making power, the enforcement power and the oversight power, and in such a leadership system, it is difficult for powers to be reasonably broken down and restrained by each other.

The standing committees of the Party Committee at all levels are generally comprised of the top leaders of the Party affairs system, People's Congress, Political Consultative Conference and government. As the central leader, the standing committee of the Party Committee has the function of collective decision-making; upon the collective decision-making, the members of the standing committee will carry out their own duties, and the standing committee also takes care of the supervision over the enforcement results. The inner-party supervision, the People's Congress's supervision, and the Political Consultative Conference's supervision are all carried out under the leadership of the Party Committee.

It is also the combination of legislative and executive powers that is practiced by the People's Congress. As the organ with the supreme power in the legal principle, the People's Congress has the legislative power, power of appointment and removal of personnel, decision-making power over significant matters, and oversight power. It is both the lawmaker and supervisor, and has its own enforcement authority.

The power distribution structure of the three-power combination makes it impossible to carry out the external supervision of faulty decision-making or the supervision over the enforcement power. It is a dictatorial power lacking checks and balances and all powers are gathered either in one institution or in one individual, which creates the possibility of power abuse.

Fourth, there is no effective legal guarantee for supervision of media

Presently, the media management system of China is more prior review than subsequent punishment, stresses more the media's functions of positive publicity and opinion guidance than the function of criticism and supervision, and relies upon more policy documents, administrative intervention and power of personnel appointment and removal than the management based on law, and features more forbidding standards than protective standards for media. Owing to the absence of such basic laws that are essential to the existence and development of media as the *Media Law* and *Media Tort Liability Law*, the media freedom cannot be guaranteed by legal means, and there is no law to protect the right of public opinion supervision. The effect of supervision by public opinions is mostly determined by whether leaders of different levels support the supervision by public opinions and how great is that support. And the effect of network supervision is mostly determined by whether the leaders and cadres of different levels and special supervision authorities pay attention and give response.

Fifth, the low level of the democratic construction of governance by law has limited the growth space for election accountability and the mechanism of checks and balances between powers.

Since the reform and opening up, although China has made efforts in the construction of democracy and governance by law for over 30 years, the realization of democracy and governance by law remains at a low level.

A free and competitive direct election system is the foundation of democratic politics. So far, except for the election of representatives of the People's Congress, which can be practiced at as high a level as the county, district and municipal levels, the direct election of Party and government leaders is still confined to the village level. The multi-candidate election is still confined to the election of deputies and somewhat a kind of "accompanying election," leaving little room for necessary competitive and free choice. The top-down appointment system remains the main channel for the power conference, and the top-down supervision and accountability system remains the most powerful accountability tool. The oversight power great number of representatives, non-professionalism, over short session, etc. There is no restraint between the legislative power, judicial power and administrative power. The localized and administrative judiciary hampers just judiciary. There is no system of judicial examination or examination of violations of constitution in the law and regulation system. The external supervision of the ruling party is far from being satisfactory.

These serious defects in the construction of democracy and governance by law for the present period have limited the growth space for election accountability and the mechanism of checks and balances between powers.

Modern Transition of the Anti-Corruption System

It is an urgent task in anti-corruption and power supervision to deepen the political system reform and realize the modern transition of China's present national anti-corruption system.

It is the central part in constructing a modern national anti-corruption system and a key link in preventing and punishing corruptions effectively to complete the vertical and horizontal mechanism of power accountability and bring power supervision and restraint in a closed circle through deepening the political system reforms.

To foster and develop a civil society and strengthen the civil society's checks and balances of the state regime is the basic approach to prevent the national politics from overriding the civil society and enjoying the power free of supervision and restraints. The most effective method for the civil society for checks and balances of the state is the right of election owned by the citizens. Through free and competitive elections held on a regular basis, citizens may force the leaders who are corrupt or abuse power to step down in a peaceful and rational way, so as to construct a strong vertical accountability system in which the state and the leaders are made to be truly accountable to society and the citizens. This kind of election accountability system cannot be replaced with any other accountability tool. Therefore, it is necessary to promote election democracy and realize the transition from to direct election.

To implement the checks and balances system within the regime authorities and make each power separated from and restrained by each other is an effective approach to prevent the power of the ruling party from growing too big to be restrained and ending up with abuse. It is pointed out in the report of the Seventeenth National Congress of the CPC that we should "establish a sound structure of power and a mechanism for its operation in which decision-making, enforcement and oversight powers check each other and function in coordination," which has defined the direction for constructing the system of checks and balances with Chinese characteristics.

Party committee, government, People's Congress, non-Communist parties and the Political Consultative Conference at each level should reasonably divide and define their own duties and functions and create dependence and restraint between all types of powers as in personnel and policy proposal, participant deliberation, examination, enforcement, deliberation, investigation and adjustment.

As the decision-maker, the Party Committee has the power of personnel and policy proposal, and power of policy and personnel adjustment. This guarantees the Party Committee's leadership as the decision-maker and coordinator.

As a kind of checks and balances of the decision-making power, non-communist parties and the Political Consultative Conference should have the participation power and speech power, i.e. participant deliberation power, on the Party Committee's decisions, and the People's Congress should have the deliberation veto power as to the policies and acts presented by the Party Committee through the government. This is essential to ensure the correctness of decisions and prevent the abuse of decision-making power.

With the power of policy enforcement, the government is an important body for exercising public powers. As a kind of checks and balances of the enforcement power, non-communist parties and the Political Consultative policies, and the deliberation result should serve as an important reference for the Party Committee to revise policies and adjust personnel arrangements.

The People's Congress should have the powers of investigation and oversight of the policies and budgets. Meanwhile, in order to improve the professionalism and effects of the powers of investigation and oversight, it is necessary to relegate the administrative monitoring authority and auditory authority to the People's Congress, making the administrative monitoring authority accept the public's petitions and complaints and investigate and deal with administrative malpractices under the leadership of the People's Congress, and making the auditory authority carry out independent audits of the administrative body and other public power bodies on behalf of the People's Congress and report the audit results to the People's Congress.

Please refer to Fig.1 for the operation of the work flow of the checks and balances mechanism as stated above.

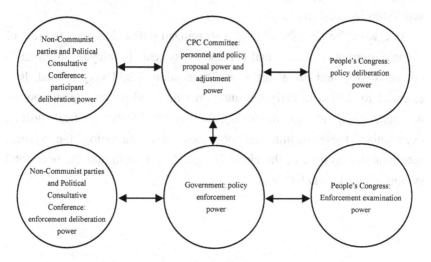

Fig. 1 Work flow of the mechanism of checks and balances: decision-making power, enforcement power, and oversight power

Source: Prepared by the author based on relevant data.
Drawing by: Chen Lei

in the process of deliberation and investigation is a core rule for the People's Congress to exercise the oversight power effectively. To confer the members of the Political Consultative Conference with the power of immunity of speech during the process of participant deliberation is the core rule for the Political Consultative Conference to exercise the oversight power effectively. This design of a checks and balances system not only guarantees the leadership of the Party Committee, but also reinforces the People's Congress and the Political Consultative Conference in exercising the power of overseeing the powers of decision-making and enforcement. It also does not weaken the government's enforcement power at the same time. So it is the system in which all three parties win and in which there are little obstacles and it is accepted by all parties.

When the checks and balances mechanism is functioning efficiently, the dependence on special supervision authorities will be greatly weakened in terms of power oversight and restraint. Meanwhile, it will become less necessary to strengthen the functions and powers of special supervision authorities in anti-corruption.

In a word, being affected by the centralized political system, the role of China's current national anti-corruption system is played in quite a restrained way and the effect of anti-corruption is still very limited. It is essential for China to carry out anti-corruption and power supervision for the next stage through deepening the reform of the political system, overcoming these institutional obstacles, and improving the vertical accountability system in the citizen's right for election and the horizontal system of checks and balances.

12

China in the Next 30 Years:

Deepening Economic Reform from the Man-Nature Relationship

Wang Songpei

Wang Songpei

Honorary department member, researcher, professor and senior editor of the China Academy of Social Sciences. He is a renowned ecological economist of China, the forerunner, founder and theoretical co-founder of the ecological economics of China, and also an academic leader. He has been dedicated to the research of the establishment and development of China's socialist rural economics for 60 years and new discipline research of ecological economics for 30 years. For a long time, he was Vice Chairman and Secretary General of the China Ecological Economics Society and Director of Research Center for Eco-Environmental Sciences, Chinese Academy of Sciences, chairing the research and promotion of China's ecological economics. He is presently President of the China Institute of Eco-Environmental Sciences and a Chief Expert of the World Ecological Economics Institute.

"The deepening of reform from the man-nature relationship for the next 30 years will necessarily be a comprehensive reform in all spheres, including economy, society, culture and politics."

—*Wang Songpei*

It has been 30 years since China began to shift its focus on economic construction and launched the economic reform in 1979. Over the past 30 years, China has, as guided by Deng Xiaoping's theory, achieved a remarkable success by carrying out economic reform from the man-man relationship. Presently, China's economic and social development has entered a new eco-era. The new practice in the new era has raised new requirements on China's economic development and reform, that is, to deepen economic reform from the man-nature relationship. This is a historical mission given by the new era in China, featuring great historical and practical significances. The core of further reform requires people to correctly understand and deal with the fundamental relationships in the following three aspects through combining the theory and practice of the contemporary economic and social development.

It Is Required by the New Era to Deepen the Economic Reform from the Man-Nature Relationship

The central part is to require people to correctly understand and deal with the relationship between the economic development and ecological protection from the perspective of the new era.

When the development of man's society came about at the end of the 1960s, the five explosive problems of inharmonious relationship between ecology and economy had been notably presented, i.e. the problems with population, food, resource, energy and environment throughout the world. Hence, a world environment and development campaign was launched, which has lasted for over 40 years up to now. The "United Nations Conference on the Human Environment" held in Stockholm, the capital of Sweden, in 1972 guided the countries all over the world to take actions to protect the eco-environment that had been suffering damage. However, the practice over the past 20 years after the conference has proved that it is impossible to protect the eco-environment merely through "protecting the environment for the sake of protection," which was separate from economic and social development. Therefore, the UN convened the "Conference on

Environment and Development" in Rio de Janeiro, Brazil in 1992, where the guiding concept that "environment protection must be combined with development" was formulated and the important guideline of "sustainable development" was explicitly proposed, leading man's society onto a road of overall and correct development.

From the idea of "one-sided environment protection" to the concept that "environment protection must be combined with development," then to the vision of realizing "sustainable development," it is a leap in understanding the laws of economic and social development. With the continuous development of social productivity, man's society has gone through two eras. One is the agricultural era in which the social productivity represented by "iron plough and cattle farming" promoted the agricultural revolution and established the agricultural society and a long-term agricultural civilization. The second is the industrial era in which the social productivity represented by "the invention of the steam engine" promoted the industrial revolution and established the industrial society and an industrial civilization which lasted for nearly 200 years. Compared to the agricultural era, the industrial era boasted highly-developed social productivity, but failed to be guided by the philosophy of harmony between ecology and the economy. Its basic characteristic was the inharmonious relationship between ecology and the economy, thus leading to the unsustainable development of the economic society. Based on the previous two eras, the new social productivity represented by "green technology" emerged, which has driven the new ecological revolution to establish a new ecological society and with which a new ecological civilization is being constructed. In this way, the development of society advances to the new eco-era.

As part of the world's economic and social development, the economic and social development of China has also entered the eco-era. The new eco-era has emerged for the purpose of eliminating the basic conflict of the industrial era, i.e. "the inharmonious relationship between ecology and the economy." Its basic feature is to realize a "harmonious relationship between ecology and the economy" and realize the sustainable development of the economic society based on this. In the past 30 years, the central part of

China's economic reform has been aimed at the problem that, for a long time, especially during the ten-year "Cultural Revolution," the role of the objective economic laws were ignored or even negated in the course of economic development and the country failed to realize due economic effectiveness. Basically, the reform was focused on changing the productive relationships and superstructures that failed to meet the needs of social productivity development, speeding up the liberation of social productivity, and then promoting the fast growth of China's economy. This is the huge success of China achieved under the guidance of Deng Xiaoping's theory on reform. Presently, China's economic and social development has entered a new era. The new practice in the new era has raised new requirements on China's economic development and reform, which also means new tasks for China's economic reform. One task is for China to continue to observe the objective economic laws and reform all the production relationships and superstructures that are not suitable for social productivity development, thus to further liberate the constrained social productivity and promote the rapid economic growth. The other task is for China to observe the objective laws of nature and reform all the production relationships and superstructures that are not suitable for natural productivity development, thus to liberate the constrained natural productivity and promote the sustainable economic growth. That is to say, the further rapid growth of China's economy should both meet the requirements of the laws of economy and the laws of nature, thus to explore the huge potential of the economy and ecology to the greatest extent. This has further utilized Deng Xiaoping's theory on reform and reflected the requirements raised by the Scientific Outlook on Development in the new historical period of China.

It Is a Fundamental Reform to Deepen the Economic Reform from the Man-Nature Relationship

It is essentially required that people correctly understand and deal with the man-nature relationship at the depth of objective reality.

In the reality of economic and social development, man exists and develops in a close relationship with nature. According to the theories of ecological economics, the "ecological economic system" is the objective supporter of man's economic activities. It is formed through the overlapping growth of the two subsystems of the "ecological system" and "economic system", so it is restrained by the two categories of objective laws, the laws of nature and the laws of economy, at the same time. For a long time in the past, people ignored and even negated the objective existence of the "ecological system" in developing the economy, and therefore were punished by the laws of nature, which were the root cause of damage to the ecological environment and unsustainable development of the economic society. Entering the new eco-era, when guided by the emerging theories on ecological economics, it is foremost to be equipped with the concept of "the dual existence of ecology and the economy," which will provide a ideological and epistemological basis for China to deepen the economic reform from the man-nature relationship in the next 30 years.

In order to further understand the importance of deepened economic reform from the man-nature relationship, it is also necessary to maintain a profound understanding that the man-nature relationship is fundamental in the economic society. Man has developed two kinds of relationships in developing economies. One is the man-man relationship, which has been clear to us for a long time. In the past 30 years, China's economic reform was actually targeted at solving the problems accumulated in this relationship, so China has achieved great success. The other one is the man-nature relationship, which has not attracted its deserved attention. The restraint on and even damage to the economic development arising from it are to be solved through deepened economic reform; and the great drive in economic development as embodied in it is to be explored and utilized efficiently. It is very important to note here that the man-nature relationship is a fundamental relationship in a developing economy, which is determined by the fact that man's existence and development rely upon the natural ecological system and such dependence is irreplaceable.

Engels used to point out that: man's needs include the need for existence, the need for enjoyment and the need for development. This argument describes the laws of the fundamental man-nature relationship as well as the sequence of the three industrial developments of the national economy. First, man's need for existence is the most fundamental need. From the first day of his life, man needs to seek means of livelihood in nature for the purpose of existence and return wastes back to nature, thus forming the relationship between man and nature. This is how the primary industry of the national economy started. Second, man needs to produce and develop division and cooperation in work in order to enjoy and develop, this forming the secondary industry and the tertiary industry. Obviously, the primary industry is about the man-nature relationship. The secondary industry is about the processing of natural products, which is also based on the man-nature relationship. The tertiary industry not only emerged and developed based on the first two industries, but also utilizes nature directly, such as tourism. Therefore, it is clear that it is also based on the man-nature relationship and there are also various issues about the man-nature relationship that needs study and resolution.

However, in the long course of economic development, man was not aware of the fundamental man-nature relationship. For example, for the past decades, the theory that "agriculture is the foundation of the national economy" was taken as a final conclusion for developing economies, which, however, presently needs updating in the new eco-era, providing a more profound understanding of its essence. For a long time in the past, it was generally believed that: agriculture provided food, industrial raw materials, labor and market for the development of industry and the national economy. It is now realized that such a belief is not profound; it is one-sided and even wrong. The major defects lie in that: first, it was a product of the wrong guiding concept in which cities were placed opposite to the rural area and industry deprived agriculture. Under such constraints, the poverty and backwardness in the rural areas and the peasants of China could not be changed, and the problems with agriculture, the farmer and the rural area that had long restrained China's economic development could not be solved. Second, it was a product of the one-sided guiding concept in the developing economy that ignored and even negated nature in the past. Under such constraints, even China's agriculture itself did not achieve harmony with nature, and it was inevitable that the foundation it provided to industry and the tertiary industry was incomplete. China's practical experience for the past decades has sufficiently proved that, in the next 30 years, it is completely necessary for China to further deepen the economic reform from the man-nature relationship on the basis of the great success that has been achieved in the economic reform from the man-man relationship.

It Is the Overall Construction of an Eco-Civilization to Deepen the Economic Reform from the Man-Nature Relationship

It is essentially required that people have a definite understanding of and deal with the relationship between economic reform and the overall reform from the interconnections in the economic and social development. Hence, according to the theories of ecological economics, in the economic and social development, all kinds of economies and the development of economy, society, culture and politics is an integrated whole in which they are closely connected with and are promoted by each other. The economic activities carried out by people will necessarily evolve to economic and social activities. Hence, as the supporter of the basic relationship of social development (ecology-economy relationship), the "ecological economic system" will necessarily be expanded to a more complex "ecological-economic-social system." Therefore, the deepened economic reform of China in the next 30 years will necessarily promote the deepened reform in the spheres of the economy, society, culture and politics simultaneously from the man-nature relationship.

For a start, let us look at the deepening of reform in the economic sphere. It is going to be an overall reform ranging from the way of thinking and guiding concept to production and specific management from the man-nature relationship for the next 30 years. For instance, it may include: (1) developing a new thought of the eco-era, i.e., the thought of the dual existence of the economy and ecology, the thought of harmony between the economy and ecology, and the thought of sustainable development of the economic society; (2) formulating a new strategic guiding concept, i.e. the strategic guiding concept of "harmony between the economy and ecology"; (3) establishing a new guideline and policies for developing economies, e.g. the policies on production, distribution, circulation and consumption for harmony between the economy and ecology; (4) establishing a new scientific and technological system for harmony between the economy and ecology, i.e. the green technology system; (5) establishing a new management system for harmony between the economy and ecology, i.e. the green management system; etc. Of all those aspects, those remarkably significant reform issues that are listed for focused research include:

First, to deepen the reform of the economic system from the man-nature relationship. It is necessary to study and establish "a socialist market economy oriented in the ecological economy."

Second, to deepen the reform of the pattern of economic growth from the man-nature relationship. It is necessary to set up "an ecological-economy-intensive pattern of economic growth."

Third, to deepen the reform of economic development model from the man-nature relationship. It is necessary to study the transformation from the previous economic model "oriented in quantity and speed" to the one "oriented in economic efficiency," then to the economic model "oriented in the efficiency of the ecological economy."

Fourth, to deepen the reform of economic behaviors from the man-nature relationship. It is necessary to study the inner coordination between the present benefits and long-term benefits, and overcome various short-term economic behaviors, including those in terms of production targets, utilization of natural resources, management of cadres' performance, and so on.

Then, let us see the deepening of reform in the full-range sphere of the economy and society. The deepening of reform from the man-nature relationship for the next 30 years will necessarily be a comprehensive reform in all spheres, including the economy, society, culture and politics. Throughout the development of man's society, the economic relationship is the fundamental one. This is because economic activities are the basic activities of mankind. However, when people carry out economic activities and form certain economic relationships, they are at the same time engaged in certain types of social, cultural and political activities, hence necessarily developing certain social, cultural and political relationships. These relationships are created and going on at the same time with the economic relationship, so essentially, they consist of both a man-man relationship and a man-nature relationship. Therefore, when they are reformed from the man-man relationship, it is also necessary to deepen the reform from the man-nature relationship, thus to base the further development of China's economic society on both harmony between man and man and harmony between man and nature, i.e. to realize the overall harmony of economic society.

Looking deeper, it will be found that the process in which China carries out the reform of its ecological economy is essentially a process of constructing an ecological civilization. Civilization is the fruits of man's economic, social, cultural and political development in total; it refers to the total material and spiritual fruits that have been gained by mankind from adapting to the world (including the world of man and the world of nature) and changing the world, and also the general symbol of advancement of man's society. And the ecological civilization is the total material and spiritual fruits that have been gained by mankind through understanding the new requirements of the eco-era and observing the objective laws of developing the economic society with "harmony between ecology and the economy." The eco-era is a brand new era, and the ecological civilization is the supreme civilization in man's history. In the past 30 years, the economic reform launched by China through observing the objective economic laws from the man-man relationship greatly promoted the rapid development of China's economic society and won China a huge success. In the next 30 years, it is certain that China is also going to achieve a great success in the reform of the ecological economy by observing the objective laws of the ecological economy from the man-nature relationship, thus to drive China's economic society to go ahead on the road of sustainable development.

13

What Should We Learn from China

Josef Gregory Mahoney

Josef Gregory Mahoney
Professor of Politics and Director of the International Graduate Program in
Politics at East China Normal University in Shanghai, Associate Editor of
the Journal of Chinese Political Science, Editor of the Fudan Journal of the
Humanities and Social Sciences, Associate Editor of ECNU Review and
regular columnist for Beijing Review. Additionally, his publications have
appeared in numerous leading Chinese and Western journals, including
Marxism and Reality, Foreign Theoretical Trends, The Journal of Studies in
Mao Zedong Thought and Deng Xiaoping Theory, Science & Society, TSLA,
The China Journal, and Rethinking Marxism, among others. He was
formerly a Senior Researcher with the Central Compilation and Translation
Bureau (Beijing) and a member of the Chinese team that translated Jiang
Zemin's Selected Works into English.

Introduction

Today's topic is, "What we should learn from China?" This is a very important topic for all of us here today and it is an increasingly important topic for people around the world. As most of you already know, many developing countries are seeking alternatives to Western development strategies and philosophies based on neoliberalism, the so-called "Washington Consensus," a hegemonic American dollar, and so on. Therefore, it is unsurprising that an open-minded and receptive trend exists with respect to China and new ideas. For too many years, people listened very closely to the United States and Europe; but today, people are seeking alternatives because they recognize the West as having entered a period of relative decline. They see that many Western ideas have led to environmental, economic, and political crises. History is quite clear already on these points. For example, after the Soviet Union fell, Russia adopted many Western economic and political ideas, leading disastrously to both chaos and an elitist oligarchy. Unfortunately, the Russian example is not unique. Other countries have suffered under the Western model over the last twenty to thirty years. China, however, has resisted. To be sure, China embarked on relatively radical reforms including introducing and developing a socialist market economy and the like, and further, as everyone knows, China's reform and development still has a lot of work ahead of it. Nevertheless, while others have been falling, China has been rising. So this has led some people to ask if there is something that we should learn from China.

Nevertheless, regardless of their education and training, regardless of their good intentions and fine personalities, many people are not really well prepared intellectually or psychologically to ask this question, let alone try to answer it. A famous Western political scientist gave a talk a couple of years ago in Beijing at the Central Compilation and Translation Bureau. Let me say that he is a personal friend of mine and indeed, is one of my former professors, and he is by far one of the nicest and most diligent scholars I have ever met. Nevertheless, he has studied China for almost the entire reform period, and like a lot of Western researchers, he has a strong bias against the Chinese political system, insomuch as he views it negatively compared to Western liberalism. The most compelling comment he made during his talk in Beijing was the following: "All contemporary Western models of political science and economics predict that China, and specifically, the Chinese government, must fail. And yet, it has not failed." He conceded that while he could not figure out why the Chinese government has not failed, in his opinion, surely it must. So we must ask here today: Is it not interesting that a leading Western scholar would come to China to do research, ostensibly to "learn from China," and yet, is perhaps so incapable of setting aside his own Western biases that in fact, he is less interested in "learning from China" than puzzling over why China has not learned from and copied the West? In other words, why has China not become more Western in its political system or, at least, failed according to Western predictions? It is not remarkable that intelligent people are still thinking this way despite all the evidence and crises that surround them? Unfortunately, this scholar's opinions are not unique among his Western colleagues. All the same, his thinking again begs the question: "What should we learn from China?"

Epistemes and Epistemological Ruptures and Shifts

Anyone with even a basic understanding of Chinese history understands that countries rise and fall, and if history is long enough, as China's surely is, then they have probably risen and fallen many times. There are many reasons why countries if not regions and cultures rise and fall, but it is clear that, whether a direct cause or merely a correlation, "rising and falling" is generally accompanied by changes in terms of what and how people think.

A lot has been written over the years about such phenomenon, with the famous philosopher of science Thomas Kuhn describing such changes in his book, *The Structure of Scientific Revolutions* (1962), as "paradigm shifts." I mention Kuhn's concept here because many if not all of you are probably familiar with it, but in fact, I am more interested in discussing a similar but somewhat different concept from the equally if not more famous French thinker, Michel Foucault, who in his books *The Order of Things* (1966) and *The Archeology of Knowledge* (1969) discussed at length what he termed "epistemes," i.e., a relatively specific period of time defined in terms of what and how people thought, and "epistemological ruptures," i.e., a break in the old ways of thinking and knowing, preceding the emergence of a new episteme, i.e., a new period defined by new ways of thinking and new knowledge.

First, however, let us review a basic definition of epistemology so we can have a firmer grasp of what Foucault had in mind. Epistemology is the study of knowledge, where the object of study is "knowledge" itself. In other words, epistemology is concerned with questions like, "what do we know" and "how do we know what we know" and "why do we think this way," etc. Of course, epistemology is not just concerned with present knowledge. Scholars in this field are particularly interested in different ways of thinking and knowing through history, across different cultures, of how ways of thinking and knowing change, and further, how they change across cultures and indeed, how they change people and vice versa. On the one hand, it may seem like a rather abstract if not theoretical field, but on the other hand, we can and will illustrate very specific historical and contemporary examples of such changes in this lecture. Some brief examples here may prove helpful. As you know, not so long ago in China and indeed, around the world, many people believed erroneous and harmful things about women. Thankfully, although some foolish people still think that way, many people have changed their thinking about women and as a result, women have been able to reach new heights in some countries and cultures around the world. Here's another example. Just over a century ago, many Chinese believed in some form or another that the emperor was the "son of heaven." This way of thinking influenced the way they thought about many things, not just government. Over time, there was a change, and today, there is no emperor and indeed, very few if any who believe that any emperor was ever truly the "son of heaven." With these two examples in mind we can understand the following.

First, the study of ways of thinking and knowing is called epistemology. And second, when significant changes in how people think and what they know occur, it is sometimes appropriate to describe such changes as "epistemological ruptures" that result in epistemological shifts. Thus, Foucault's concepts will be helpful for us here, as will those of another French thinker, Louis Althusser. Let us make a brief note here that while Foucault derives a lot of his thinking from Friedrich Nietzsche, in fact, at the center of our discussion we will find ideas and concepts that are in fact familiar to Karl Marx, V.I. Lenin, and Mao Zedong.

Let us now look more deeply at some of Foucault's ideas about knowledge. According to Foucault, as we have already alluded, human history is made up of different time periods, during which people believed different things. Foucault calls these different periods "epistemes." Etymologically, therefore, it is clear that Foucault defines different periods in terms of different forms of knowledge and different ways of thinking. We have already given the example of the "emperor as the son of heaven," and in fact, Foucault points to a similar example in his own work looking at the French Revolution. Before the Revolution, many believed the monarch enjoyed what was called the "divine right of kings," a right that people thought was derived from God. However, the Revolution indicates a significant rupture in this way of thinking, insomuch as the French masses in fact overthrew and executed Louis XVI in 1793. In other words, before the French Revolution, most people believed that the king was king because God wanted him to be king; but after the Revolution, people no longer believed this, and there was therefore an epistemic break and a shift, one where people began to believe different things. Of course, this shift was not just concerned about politics. It was also concerned with people's thinking about God and many other areas of thought.

According to Foucault, the change from one episteme to the next is generally not a process of slow evolution. Rather, it is more like a revolution, one that commonly follows a dramatic rupture, and yet, every revolution has distinct stages, he argues, and further, even if a relatively quick, revolutionary rupture emerges, progressing through these stages may still take time. Indeed, not every revolution is successful, regardless of the initial rupturing, revolutionary event. Let us keep in mind here that Foucault is talking specifically about epistemic revolutions, and that he is doing so by focusing on the emergence of new discourses and discursive developments. Thus, when Foucault theorizes that an epistemic shift reaches its most complete state generally speaking after crossing four thresholds, he means that the discourse has advanced in some way through four stages. He describes the four thresholds as follows: Crossing the first threshold, "positivity," means that a new way of thinking (which we can understand is a type of discourse) has emerged and thus been accepted affirmatively by some as offering a new if not alternative knowledge. Crossing the second threshold, "epistemologization," means that this new discourse has taken its place systematically as a discourse in the world of ideas and values and likely, has begun to dominate relative to other ideas. In the third stage, "scientificity," the new discourse has begun to create its own rules and regulations and in some sense, its own grammar and vocabulary, insomuch as it is a discourse. In the fourth stage, "formalization," the new discourse completes its formal development and offers what it considers to be a full set of principles, methods, and so on.

We have already mentioned Thomas Kuhn, whose work examined revolutionary shifts in scientific thinking in Western history. For example, for a long time, many in the West believed in Aristotelian physics. However, with the development of Newtonian physics, there was a paradigm shift away from Aristotelian physics, and again, with the development of Einstein's theories, there was a shift away from many of Newton's ideas. It is easy to see, I think, and further, easy to understand the significance of such changes in terms of scientific study and knowledge. It is easy in part because we can see today that certain ancient ways of thinking about the physical world were obviously incorrect, and we can know this because we can compare what the ancients knew about the physical world with what we know today and understand what were the mistakes in their understanding. Additionally, it is easy to see that such changes are not limited to science alone. Such changes can impact many aspects of human life and the natural world, including religion, politics, economics, education, environmental development and so on, and therefore, trying to understand such changes is vital for thinking intelligently about the past, present and future.

As educators, the fact that such changes occur should both thrill and frighten us. On the one hand, is it not thrilling that new ways of understanding are produced, that there are new things to learn and teach, that help us advance and that help us help others in turn? And yet, is it not frightening to think that some if not much of what we now teach so confidently is, should, or will be passé? Or that some of what we take positively as new knowledge in fact might be incorrect or even, harmful to progress? I raise these points specifically because, as this talk suggests, I believe we may be entering or more likely, have already entered a period of significant change, perhaps a revolutionary period, epistemologically speaking, and that we are already confronted by such challenges, whether we know it or not. That such changes and challenges occur periodically is a well-established historical fact, and we can see historical evidence of such changes going back over thousands of years. Our point here is that there are signs today that we are once again in such a period. I will elaborate more on this a little later, as this is a central concern for our talk as a whole: that the Western epistemological tradition has enjoyed a near hegemonic, global position for some time now, but there are indications that this tradition is in decline while a number of alternatives seem to be emerging. Chief among these alternatives, I would argue, are those being cultivated in China.

But first, we need to cover another theoretical concept here before we can really make sense of historical trends and the arguments that follow them. Therefore we turn now to Louis Althusser's famous essay "Contradiction and Overdetermination," which assesses the Bolshevik Revolution from both a Leninist and Maoist perspective. Drawing from Mao Zedong, Althusser recognizes that a successful revolution requires many factors or contradictions working in favor of revolution, and that these contradictions are themselves "particular" and "uneven" with respect to the specific material conditions that the revolutionary movement faces. Then, Althusser turns to Lenin's assessment that the Bolshevik Revolution succeeded because Russia presented the "weakest link" in the chain of modern bourgeois nations. Lenin saw that Russia was simultaneously "the most backward and the most advanced nation" and the "weakest link" given its manifold contradictions and its historical context, he saw that a number of contradictions fuse critically into a "ruptural unity" against which no real defense is possible, a lesson in part derived also from Mao. Then, given these conditions and opportunities, an organization like the parties led by Lenin and Mao could, through critical praxes, become the most advanced and irrepressible agents for change.

For the moment, let us keep these theoretical concepts in mind as we look at a number of espistemological shifts over the history of the Western experience before examining how these theories might help us think about ongoing changes in China and the West and further, how these theories might help us think about our titular question. We must begin with looking critically at the Western epistemological tradition because the truth is, for more than a century, China has looked beyond its own borders for new knowledge and practices. While China has certainly contributed to global knowledge throughout all of human history and certainly in the last century, it is fair to say that since the Xinhai Revolution and at least the May Fourth Era, the Chinese experience has been one that has been marginalized significantly by a hegemonic Western, including Soviet, epistemological tradition.

What Does the West Know and How Does it Know?

The contemporary Western episteme has been influenced, of course, by many sources, past and present. Let us raise a quick question that some of you might have. When I speak here of a "Western episteme," can we speak of a single way of thinking or type of thinking? For example in the West, to illustrate the problem here, we find many different ideas and traditions, so it can be somewhat difficult to say specifically what the West is in terms of a particular episteme. Nonetheless, we can speak of a Western episteme where certain ideas and values are hegemonic, i.e., ideas that have more power and privilege than other ideas, which are central to many prevailing aspects of Western thinking and acting. And these ideas and traditions include the philosophy of individualism, basic positive and positivistic ideas about capitalism and bourgeois democracy, Judeo-Christian but especially Protestant morality, the "end of history," and so on.

Let us start with the Greeks and specifically, let us begin with the example of Socrates and then continue with one of the more famous narratives from Western philosophy, Plato's "Allegory of the Cave." So here is a simple question: Was Socrates a good or bad person? In the West, in fact, Socrates is seen as one of the greatest heroes. But let us consider for a moment that Socrates was in fact a bad guy. After all, he was accused of crimes against society, and was tried, convicted and executed by his fellow citizens, so it seems prudent that we consider that he was, perhaps, not the best of men. We must examine, why was Socrates executed, and further, who executed him?

First, when Socrates was alive, Athens was, for the most part, a democracy. Of course, it was not some idealized people's democracy, and certainly, suffrage and related political rights were very limited. Nevertheless, many Athenians were rather pleased with their political system, which they viewed as being positively distinctive from the political practices of other Greek city-states and non-Greek realms. At one point, however, a group that became known as the "Thirty Tyrants" overthrew the Athenian government and ruled rather ruthlessly for a period of time before democracy was restored. Some of the "Thirty" were Socrates' former students. After the tyrants were overthrown, some Athenian's speculated, rightly or wrongly, that Socrates was in some way responsible for the tyrants' beliefs.

Second, when the "Thirty" seized control, a lot of Athens' leading citizens fled the city and did not return until the democratic government had been restored. Socrates' did not leave the city, however, and further, the "Tyrants did not persecute him" although some who did remain faced violence. Therefore, some saw Socrates as supporting the "Tyrants" or vice versa.

Third, after democracy was restored, Socrates continued teaching like before. Some felt that he should have made some changes in terms of his pedagogy and the content of his philosophy. They believed he had "corrupted the youth of Athens" and that he was continuing to do so, and thus, he had this charge brought against him.

Fourth, insomuch as Athens was a democracy, Socrates was given a democratic trial. When he was confronted with the charge against him, Socrates defended himself in part by elaborating on his own critical intelligence and abilities and the moral need to cultivate the same in his students, regardless of the broader sociological consequences. Unsurprisingly, when the jury heard this defense, it voted and found Socrates guilty. When Socrates was asked to suggest his punishment, he claimed that being guilty of such a crime should be rewarded with high honors, and thus, he was seen as mocking the city, its people, and its institutions. Again, unsurprisingly, the Athenian jury voted and Socrates was sentenced to death.

Now let us ask. Was Socrates a good or bad man? On the one hand, if you are opposed to democracy, then you might consider Socrates to be a good man. Likewise, if you are devoted to individual, critical advancement, you might think he is good as well. On the other hand, if you believe that democracy is valuable for the greater good, and further, that knowledge should serve the greater good, then you are likely to view Socrates less favorably.

Why are we discussing Socrates here? The answer is rather simple. Many Westerners admire Socrates for standing up against the government, for being the radical individual, for teaching his students to think critically. Many in the West admire Socrates' famous quote during his trial as written by Plato in the Apology, "the unexamined life is not worth living." This quote has echoed throughout Western history in a variety of ways. The American revolutionary, Patrick Henry, for example, famously shouted "Give me liberty or give me death" in 1765, while Nathan Hale, an American revolutionary soldier, told his British captors "I only regret that I have but one life to lose for my country" before he was hanged in 1776. Socrates' example as well as these from Henry and Hale illustrate some of the paradoxical and conflicting values at the heart of Western thinking, namely, the values of individualism, elitism, democracy, justice, critical thinking, social responsibility, and so on.

These paradoxes are also found in the "Allegory of the Cave," one of the most famous passages found in Plato's book *The Republic*. Like the example of Socrates, most students in the West today are taught that the "Allegory" is a noble, positive story, one that shows how one becomes educated and how one can rise through education and hard work. While many of you are probably familiar with the "Allegory," it is a good idea to review it briefly. Plato describes a deep cave, and in the deepest part, people are chained like prisoners and held in place. They can only see the wall of the cave, directly in front of them. They cannot move, they cannot turn around, that cannot see what is happening behind them. They can only look directly ahead. Somewhere behind them, however, is a fire, and between the fire and the prisoners a "parade" of things, objects, people, and whatnot marches back and forth. The light from the fire casts shadows on the wall of the cave in front of the prisoners, who then try to discern what they are seeing based on the shadows. It is a guessing game, one that is made difficult by the dancing light of the fire, the movement of the objects, the restrictions on the prisoners, and so on, and likewise, we can surmise, the smoke from the cave as well as the prisoners' general ignorance predisposes them to make all sorts of mistakes. Nevertheless, some of the prisoners become "leaders," or perhaps "prophets" is a better description, insomuch as their guessing becomes respected by others.

One day, however, a prisoner breaks free and can begin to move. At first, perhaps, the prisoner's muscles are atrophied and likewise, the prisoner is probably frightened by his new condition. His confidence builds, however, and as he explores the cave, he learns the truth that was otherwise obscured behind him. His strength and determination builds, and he decides he wants to know more. He discovers the tunnel leading out of the cave, and at the end of the tunnel, he discerns a glimmer of sunlight. Although he is still weak and the rough, rocky path wounds him, he struggles forward anyway and reaches the mouth of the cave. As he steps outside, he is blinded by the light of the sun. After his eyes adjust, he begins to explore the world around him. He experiences all the wonders that were previously only suggested by shadows. He enjoys the sunlight and the clean air, he enjoys, frankly, the "truth."

What happens next? It is very nice to be outside the cave, of course, but after some time, there is the nagging conviction that he must return to the cave and try to save some of the other prisoners. He does not want to go back, of course, because the cave is both a terrible and dangerous place to be. There are people in the cave who do not want to be free, and there are also people there who do not want him to help others. If he goes back, they might kill him. Nevertheless, he goes back to the cave to work as a teacher, as a liberator, and his fate is uncertain.

Although Plato wrote this story, it is narrated in *The Republic* by a character rendition of Socrates. In this way, Plato conveys in part his conviction that Socrates was the teacher and Athens was the cave, and in part, we can understand that Plato saw himself as having been rescued by Socrates who, as many of you know, was one of Plato's teachers.

There is another point here, one that we should note, namely, that in Plato's philosophy, once a person truly knows the Truth, then that knowledge compels one to live by the Truth. In another word, once you really know the truth, you must teach others, you must try to help them reach the "light," regardless of the consequences. In fact, this story, however told by Plato, is a common one in the West. Plato wrote the "Allegory" long before Jesus or the rise of Christianity, and we can find that the Christians appropriated the Platonic tradition. In fact, the story of Jesus is very similar to the "Allegory." Like the "Allegory" and further, like the example of Socrates, Jesus was a teacher who taught ideas and concepts that were considered contrary to local if not imperial laws and values. Jesus considered himself to be a teacher who was trying to save non-believers from ignorance, from the cave of darkness if not Hell. Like Socrates, Jesus was tried, convicted and executed, and was buried in a cave. Three days later, according to the Christian tradition, Jesus rose from the dead and continued preaching before ascending through the light, up to heaven.

There are many similarities between these two stories and many others. We will look at another important one from the Western tradition, this one coming from Paul, who some consider a saint and an apostle of Jesus. Paul was originally a Jewish man and Roman citizen named Saul, and it was his job to persecute Christians. One day, while on the road to Damascus, Saul was confronted by a vision of a resurrected Jesus, an experience that blinded him. For three days, Saul could not see, a parallel to the three days Jesus supposedly spent in the cave where he was buried after being crucified. To this experience, Saul attributes his conversion from Judaism to Christianity, and upon becoming a Christian; he changed his name to Paul.

Paul famously described himself as a "Jew by birth, a Christian by faith, a citizen by Rome, a Greek by education." As you know, Rome had conquered Greece and assimilated Greek philosophy, art, and teaching, and had even accepted Greek gods after giving them Roman names. This sort of assimilation is relatively common in history. In China, for example, the Western Zhou carried forward many of the advances made by the Shang, the Yuan built on its predecessors and became "Chinese," and so on. The Romans, in a sense, became Greek, particularly in the fields of education and knowledge. Thus, when Paul describes himself as a Greek in terms of his education, what he is saying is that he was in fact familiar with Plato's philosophy and indeed, familiar with the "Allegory of the Cave." Is it not fitting then that his conversion experience has its narrative roots in the examples described by Plato and Jesus, and further, that like Socrates and Jesus, according to tradition, Paul was charged, tried, convicted, and executed for acts against the state?

Now let us move on to the story of Augustine, Bishop of Hippo in North Africa, an early leader of the Roman Catholic Church, who some refer to as a "saint" and who the Church calls its first theologian. Augustine lived during the waning days of the Roman Empire. During Paul's time, as we have already discussed, Christianity was still a fringe religion, one that was persecuted by Rome. By Augustine's time, however, Christianity had become Rome's official state religion. We do not have time here to discuss how this dramatic change came. The key point is that over time, the Church became stronger and stronger while the state became weaker and weaker. Some people believe there's a correlation between these changes, that the Church getting stronger had a weakening affect on the state. While there is arguably some truth to such thinking, in fact, there were many factors leading to the fall of Rome. When we say that Augustine was the Church's first major theologian, what we want to convey is that Christian beliefs, principles, and practices in the early years of the Church were a rough hodgepodge. Augustine, who became a Christian after his own conversion experience, and who, like Paul, had been educated according to Rome's Greco educational and philosophical values, observed two important facts. First, he observed that Paul was influenced significantly by Greek philosophy, particularly Plato, and further, that the Bible, the bulk of which had been written by Paul, was likewise influenced by Platonic thinking. This realization gave Augustine the idea that much of Plato's thinking and logic could and should be used to structure and make sense of Church thinking.

We have reached now, a very important and rarely observed aspect of Western history, one that speaks volumes about the Western epistemological tradition. When Augustine began to "Christianize" Platonic thinking, he did so in part as a means for solidifying Christian thinking. In a sense here, we could trace the development of Christianity in terms of how it crosses Foucault's different thresholds. Augustine, in a sense, represents the fourth stage, where Christianity is formalized. But when a way of thinking reaches a position like the one attained by Christianity, and indeed, when it becomes formalized like it was under Augustine, then what we usually observe is a way of thinking that has become hegemonic and dominating, and further, a way of thinking that is intolerable and oppressive. It is not surprising, therefore, that one of the early "casualties" of Augustine's Platonic theology was the demotion and eventual banning of Aristotelian thought.

If we say that Rome was "Greek" in terms of its knowledge and education, we mean that the Romans celebrated the thinking and teachings of Plato and Aristotle, along with many others. As many of you know, whereas Plato was a student of Socrates, Aristotle was a student of Plato. Nevertheless, while some aspects of Aristotle's thinking complements

Plato's philosophy, in fact, Aristotle diverges significantly. Plato was against democracy and supported the notion of a "philosopher-king" who was empowered by an unsurpassed knowledge of metaphysical truths, while Aristotle believed that some sort of aristocracy should flourish based on the empirical experiences of talented men. Suffice to say, Paul favored Platonic over Aristotelian thinking, and likewise, Augustine as well. Indeed, Plato's notion of a philosopher-king corresponded affirmatively with the concept of papal authority and rule, while Augustine's thinking did not.

It can be argued that the Roman Empire achieved its success in part because it had synthesized different ways of thinking and therefore could adjust and adapt to changing conditions. When Rome was in its waning days, however, its movement towards the Platonic tradition alone left it weaker, and all the more so given the fact that Aristotelian thinking at that time provided much of the basis for scientific thinking and knowledge. But this did not concern the Church, because according to the Church, truth could be found in the Bible, and could be learned from Church leaders. Further, according to the Church, implicitly, the real purpose of life was to reach heaven, therefore, man's advancement in material terms was seen as secondary if not contrary to his metaphysical fate. However, the physical fate of Western man at this time in history was in fact awful. As the Roman Empire collapsed, in its stead smaller kingdoms arose. However, the Church remained. The French became French, but they remained Catholic, the same for the English and so on.

This time in history was the beginning of what we now call Europe's "Dark Ages." The Church was responsible for education, responsible for teaching, but in fact, very few people had the privilege of learning and further, "true" knowledge and learning was available only to Church elites. This went on for many centuries and most Europeans suffered terribly as a result. On the Arabian Peninsula, meanwhile, a new religion arose, Islam, and the Greeks, Christians, and Jews, strangely enough, influenced these early Muslims. The Muslims valued Plato and Aristotle immensely, and in part, saw their religious mission as a correction to Christian mistakes. In fact, the Muslims accepted Jesus as a prophet, but they did not accept him as the "son of God," as the Christians did, in part because this violated the first of the "Ten Commandments," as written down by Moses, which held that there is "only one God." However, what interests us here is that, initially, the Muslims, like the Romans, successfully synthesized the Aristotelian and Platonic traditions, and further, they did so in a way that fit Arabian conditions and needs. Unsurprisingly, in a short period of time, the Arabs, newly organized and energized under a unifying religion, were able to make great advances in science and technology while rapidly expanding their empire. Of course, this took place during Europe's Dark Ages, and thus, there was a vacuum of power and technological development that opened a door, in part, for Arab development and expansion. While Arabs made contributions to math and science, Europeans forgot what they had previously known. There is a famous example of one of the Medici families in Italy at this time offering a substantial sum for any engineer who could build a dome over the family courtyard, and yet, there was no European left who knew the math or art necessary for such work. Meanwhile, the Arabs celebrated their arches, their domes, and their freestanding minarets.

We began this part of our discussion by asking, "What does the West know and how does it know it?" We have reviewed in part some of the different ways of thinking found in Western history and further, we have reached a point in our narrative where the Muslims are more advanced than the Christian Europeans. Further again, our narrative has reached a point in its historical progression where Arab expansion was coming increasingly in conflict with what had been, for some time, the Christian lands of Europe. In fact, Augustine had been a bishop in North Africa, but almost all of North Africa would fall to the Arabs. The Arabs then crossed the mouth of the Mediterranean Sea and seized large parts of Spain. Much of the beautiful architecture they built there can still be seen today. The Muslims also approached Europe from its southeast, taking the "Holy Lands" of Judaism and Christianity and approaching the heart of Europe through Turkey. The Muslims expanded through the Balkan Mountains, and as a result, as you know, Christian versus Muslim fighting continues to be a source of conflict in places like the former Yugoslavia. In Western Europe, the Muslims continued their northward advance through Spain, and some have suggested that it was only the relatively easily defended, narrow passes of the Pyrenees Mountains that limited the Muslims to the Iberian Peninsula and kept them out of France. Nevertheless, it was clear to some that the Christian position was unsustainable. Augustine's Platonic dogmatism had hamstrung European thinking and development for far too long, and the fate of European culture and civilization was threatened.

The University of Paris, which was not that far from the Muslim front, was the first to break with papal authority, and they did so by teaching Aristotelian philosophy. Because there few texts by Aristotle remained in Europe, and because the most advanced scholarship on Aristotle was being done by the Muslims, scholars from the University of Paris smuggled Aristotelian texts and related commentaries out of Muslim-controlled Spain. In fact, the proximity to the Muslim invasion offered two geographic advantages. First, obviously, the scholars in France understood directly the threat of invasion. Second, the most advanced scholarship on Aristotle at that time was being done in Spain by the Muslim scholar Ibn Rushd, who the Europeans called "Averroes." Thus, these proximities gave scholars at the University of Paris the inspiration and the content for epistemological change.

Aristotelian thinking threatened the Church and the Pope's supremacy ontologically speaking, a threat that was made worse, one can imagine, given Averroes' Islamic contextualization. Therefore, a decision had to be made with respect to either suppressing the University of Paris or finding some way to accommodate their developments. In fact, the Church chose a path that accomplished both. First, the pope tasked Thomas Aquinas with finding a way to synthesize the Church's Platonic theology with Aristotle's empirical values, and second, once this work was completed, in the form of Aquinas' masterwork, the *Summa Theologica*, it was used to re-formalize and adjudicate Church theology. Indeed, this is why Aquinas is often referred to as the Church's second "doctor," after Augustine.

These developments took place in the 13th century, but they would lay the intellectual and legal bases for the emergence of what would become known later as the "European Enlightenment." Ironically enough, Averroes in his own lifetime would be persecuted and censored, and further, the Muslim leadership would begin to abandon Aristotle and turn more exclusively towards Platonic philosophy, as the Europeans had, as a means for consolidating political power over a large empire. Some would argue that many in the Islamic sphere have not recovered, even today, from this turn towards fundamentalist metaphysics. In fact, a Muslim scholar, a good friend of mine, has repeated to me on many occasions that one can learn all that there is to know about philosophy from Plato. In terms of the broader historical significance, however, we can see that these epistemological shifts are like two ships passing each other in the night, unaware of their proximity or their movement in opposite directions. The return to Aristotle led to European advances while the turn against Aristotle led to Muslim declines.

We have suggested already that effectively synthesizing the Platonic and Aristotelian traditions is a dialectical development, and further, that doing so can produce sounder epistemological tradition for advancement as a whole. Augustine destroyed this dialectical synthesis and in fact, Aquinas did nothing to restore it. While Aquinas' works did not result in Plato's thinking being banned effectively from Europe, as Aristotle's thinking had been following Augustine, nevertheless, Aquinas placed some aspects of Aristotle's thinking on such a high pedestal, particularly Aristotelian logic, that the possibility of a true dialectic emerging was all but destroyed. Indeed, although there is much more to Aristotelian thinking than his formal logic, and while Aquinas certainly recognized this, Aquinas' over-emphasis on Aristotle's logic foreclosed the dialectic in two ways. First, Aristotle's logic was founded on three basic laws, the law of identity, the law of non-contradiction, and the law of the excluded middle, which denied the possibility of real change and fundamentally contradictory states. Indeed, this sort of thinking, in its own way, persevered the sort of absolute, metaphysical "truths" that were central to Church theology. Second, although the return of this logical form of Aristotelian thinking functioned for a while as a dialectic within the existing Platonic milieu that persisted for a period of time following publication of the *Summa Theologica*, over time, it eventually denigrated and displaced the Platonic tradition or at least, reinterpreted that tradition within the new, positivistic episteme that emerged. Indeed, it is this latter development that provided the bases for the emergence of what is today called "modern philosophy" and modernity itself in the European tradition.

What are the hallmarks of modern thinking and European modernity? In fact, this vulgar form of Aristotelianism ultimately transformed European thinking in ways that would have left Aquinas dismayed. The sort of empiricism found in Aristotelian thinking leaves little opening for metaphysical wonder and, for that matter, it does little to humble the scientific impulse, although, as modern history has shown, scientists have sometimes taken some terribly destructive paths, especially when they have lost the sort of holistic perspective offered by dialectical thinking and further, when they have no firm, communal sense of ethics and social obligation. More than this, the new modern philosophies that emerged after Aquinas increasingly emphasized individualism, and as corollaries, supported the rise of capitalism, bourgeois democracies and Protestantism.

While linear, non-dialectical thinking can be very effective for some forms of scientific advancement, drawing straight lines between destinations, demarcating clear boundaries and laws of the modern nation-state, it can likewise prove very destructive to humanity and the environment. This was not how philosophers like Rene Descartes and Immanuel Kant viewed the advance of modernity, of course. Descartes famously proclaimed, as you know, "I think, therefore I am," but we must ask, why "I" and not "we?" Why not, "We think, therefore we are?" Why does Descartes assume that he is an individual, or that thinking is in some way wholly an individual act? Later, Kant would do much in his book, the *Critique of Pure Reason*, to categorize dialectical thinking as being far inferior to what he considered to be more analytical forms. In the meantime, Protestantism spread, as did capitalism and bourgeois democracy. As you may know, the principle theological difference between Protestantism and Catholicism is that the former asserts the individual has a personal relationship with God, while the latter asserts that one's relationship to God is mediated through the Church.

With the rise of capitalism, we see the corresponding economic system of individualism, of the selling of labor power, of celebration of capitalist competition, of the rewarding of individual exploitation, and so on. And with the rise of bourgeois democracy, we see the fitting political economy of this new episteme, one where those of the higher economic classes claim and maintain a disproportionate share of political and economic power, and do so contrary fundamentally to socialistic values of community.

The first major Western thinker in the modern era to sense this problem was G.W.F. Hegel, who recognized the importance of the dialectic and tried to reintroduce it into the European epistemological tradition. Following Hegel was Marx. Marx had an even clearer understanding of Europe's intellectual deficit, and all the more so because Marx was a materialist and further, unlike Hegel, did not feel compelled to confirm the status quo. However, for the most part, both Hegel and Marx failed to bring the dialectical tradition back to the West. Indeed, it is precisely this aspect of their thinking that most Westerners categorically reject, even today.

As we hope our discussion has illustrated, epistemic shifts are hugely significant in human history and development. And we hope that we can effectively argue that the anti-dialectical, modern Western epistemological tradition, which began to establish its global hegemony with the spread of European imperialism and colonialism, and that continues for the most part to dominate thinking in many if not most corners of the globe, has reached or is starting to reach its end. To be sure, many aspects of Western thinking have been rejected and undone by Westerners themselves following various crises. For example, the famous observation that Nazism was the natural result of Enlightenment thinking led many thinkers to reassess the European tradition in the post-war years. To a certain extent, the Great Depression forced policymakers, at least for a while, to rethink economic policy and philosophy, as did the recessions of the 1970s and early 1980s. Today, of course, we are faced with increasingly dire economic and environmental conditions — conditions that are largely the product of Western thinking or at least, competition within the hegemonic Western epistemic paradigm. It is no longer radical to think that human survival as a whole requires some sort of fundamental shift in the way we think, in terms of what we know, and certainly, in terms of how we act. We cannot merely be Platonists or Aristotelians. We cannot idealize Socrates or the Cave, nor can we lionize the individual in terms of politics, economics, and religion. We must find alternatives.

What Should We Learn from China?

We now have, I think, a good context for asking our question, "What should we learn from China?" Let me clarify firstly what I mean by "we." By "we," I mean particularly anyone whose thinking is dominated by what I have described as the non-dialectical modern Western epistemological position, and this includes non-Westerners and certainly many Chinese as well. We have already noted what was already well-known, that various efforts to open to the rest of the world for over a century has done much to inseminate China with Western thinking and to some extent, bring China to heel under the Western epistemological hegemony. In fact, this has not been an altogether bad development, although some traditionalists would no doubt disagree with me here. Nevertheless, while anti-dialectical forms of Western thinking came to China, so did its dialectical forms. The early Chinese scholars who read Marx understood him insomuch as they already had a deep dialectical tradition, one that stretches back through Chinese history to the Shang Dynasty at least. Indeed, we can see evidence of dialectical thinking in how early characters were created and written by the Shang on oracle bones, and likewise, we find dialectical thinking in the Yijing, which emerged formally during the Western Zhou. We also find dialectical thinking in both Confucius and Laozi, and when Buddhism came to China from India, it only took root after the Huayan School made it more dialectical. When Leninism and Stalinism came to China, Mao Zedong offered his famous corrective, "On Contradiction," as a way to address the dialectical deficiencies in Soviet thought. Indeed, it is fair to say that perhaps every major school of thought that has originated or taken root in China has either employed from the start or developed a significant dialectical aspect. Of course, this may well explain why Marxism was "chosen" and succeeded, relatively speaking, from among the many Western alternatives that were explored following the May Fourth Movement.

To some extent, it can be argued that China synthesized the Chinese tradition with the Western epistemological tradition. Some might argue, however, that this synthesizing effort is still incomplete, and others might argue that China has either gone too far in the Western direction or not far enough. Indeed, such debates are common in China today and they are directly related to our titular question. In the middle of this debate are three facts that contend with each other. First, relatively speaking, there is the fact of China's rise. Second, also relatively speaking, there is the fact of Western decline. Third, there is the fact of growing global economic, political, environmental, and therefore humanitarian crises.

For many years, some Chinese thinkers and policymakers have adopted some aspects of Western thinking, and they have frequently done so with the qualifier, "with Chinese characteristics." This has meant that outside ideas and practices might have been adopted, but they were also adapted to fit Chinese conditions. Of course, these efforts have not always been successful, and while some of China's modern success can be attributed to these developments, we can also trace some of China's modern problems to them as well. Suffice to say that even with the best of intentions, radical epistemological changes like those experienced in China over the last century can be difficult and dangerous, and they can also be the harbingers of incredible progress. Central to such efforts has long been the question, "What should China learn from others?" But in recent years, given its success and the mounting troubles facing others, some in China and other parts of the world have started to ask, as our introduction relates, "What should we learn from China?"

Some have pointed to the political economic concept known as the "China model." In particular, some have been attracted to the idea of the China model as an alternative to what is sometimes labeled simply if not incorrectly the "Washington Consensus" and various liberal if not neoliberal political and economic practices associated with the United States, Europe, and the institutions they largely control, like the World Bank, the International Monetary Fund, and so on, and which are sometimes backed up in cases of military conflict by the United Nations, NATO, and others. Of course, in many cases, the United States has simply acted unilaterally when it comes to economic, political, and military affairs. In light of Western failures, however, and further, given the desire of many to choose their own paths, if not for ideological reasons but simply to try alternatives that might actually work locally, the idea of a China model has gained resonance.

What is the China model? Is the China model "what we would learn from China?" Many view the China model as a paradigm or set of paradigms associated with political and economic development. It is frequently described in the West rather simply, i.e., has a non-democratic political system wed to an increasingly capitalist market economy. There are many problems with this sort of characterization and indeed, many Chinese and some Western scholars over the last several years have devoted many papers to complicating and challenging such simple-mindedness. I have three things to say about the China model. First, the scholars who have worked hard to complicate simplistic notions of the model are to be applauded. Second, however, I think we should recognize the China model positively, not as a model per se, not as something that should be dissected and replicated by policymakers elsewhere, but as a new discourse, or at least, a new discursive tradition. To be sure, it is not entirely new and it has emerged from a century of praxis (实践), but it is new in terms of its ability to be discussed globally as an alternative to hegemonic practices. Third, I think we need to recognize that the China model is in fact the result of a Chinese epistemological tradition, one that, however much knowledge it has imported from the west, remains fundamentally "Chinese." And by fundamentally Chinese, I mean that the Chinese epistemological tradition is one that has long held and to this day retains a substantial dialectical perspective.

This dialectical perspective, however unconscious at times, is still a component of Chinese language and culture, as it has been for millennia. To be sure, it has changed over time but in many important ways it remains. We can see it today in language, from the word and concept of "harmony" (和), for example, and we can likewise see it in official proclamations and, arguably, policies. Some believe, however, that the dialectic is effectively dead in China today. No doubt, in some minds and perhaps even in some corners of Chinese society, the dialectic is disparaged and neglected. Nevertheless, the dialectic remains relatively strong, I think, and its presence is both a guarantor for further growth and advancement, including the corrections of past ills. When we ask, "What should we learn from China," when we focus on the best parts of Chinese culture, I believe we need to look critically but positively at the Chinese dialectical tradition, and do so within a historical context of a non-dialectical Western epistemological tradition.

I have already alluded to the Chinese government's *hexie shehui* campaign, which as we know articulates many noble ideas that, in practice, must contend more with materiality and less with nobility. I believe, however, the harmony campaign opens the door to a broader discussion about dialectics, and indeed, actually demonstrates that dialectical thinking is still alive and well in the highest levels of Chinese political power. So let us look more deeply at this concept as we continue our broader discussion here.

The Chinese concept of harmony is one of the oldest concepts of political philosophy for which we have a written record. It originated during the Shang Dynasty, at least this is what the current historical record indicates. Perhaps someday we will discover evidence showing that it is much older. Nevertheless, as far as I am concerned, coming from the Shang, it is old enough to say that it is firmly rooted in the earliest parts of recorded Chinese history. Further, the characters developed by the Shang were different from later characters, insomuch as the phonetic element of the character, in this case, grain (禾), was also linked ideographically to the overall meaning of the word. Combined with yue (龠), which was a type of musical instrument combining several differently sounding reeds but played with a single mouthpiece, the concept of harmony (龢) reflected the challenges facing a people that had traded nomadic wandering for agricultural development and social advance. As nomads, if people disagreed with each other, they could part ways or make war on the run. But as people moved to cultivating agriculture, building cities and others forms of material progress, the question of political and economic harmony became more complex. To be sure, having an adequate food supply remained a central concern, especially as the population swelled, and thus, the phonetic privilege given to grain (禾). But there were other concerns as well that were less directly connected to grain production.

Since ancient times, music has been seen as an important source of knowledge with respect to political philosophy. Confucius reputedly said that above all others, "harmony" is the most important concept to study, and further, that if one can only carefully study one of the Chinese classics, then he should focus on the *Book of Songs* (诗经). As cities grew, maintaining harmony became difficult with increasing differences and competition, especially in difficult times and uncertainty over control of resources and power. Some critics today say that Hu Jintao's discussion of harmony signals a break with Mao Zedong's discussion of contradiction (矛盾), but this sort of reductive thinking is wrong and misleading. Indeed, the concept of harmony carries the concept of contradiction in the core of its meaning. One cannot begin to understand harmony if one does not have an understanding of contradiction. The concept of harmony conveys that despite contradiction, we can still have something positive and productive if not beautiful.

Another aspect of "和" that bears noting here is the fact that it also means the common conjunction, "and." To point out the significance of this, consider the following. The Danish philosopher Søren Kierkegaard published a lengthy, two-volume book titled *Either/Or* (1843), the point which includes is substantially a lengthy diatribe against Hegelian dialectics. In other words, Kierkegaard, the father of Western existential thought, whose contemporary influence is not always direct but should not be underestimated even today, took issue with what he saw as the "and" of Hegel's inclusionary, holistic philosophy, and instead insisted that the only moral course was one that chose definitively one option or another, where one was morally superior to the other, and thus, morally contradictory, and thus, unsupportable. This sort of thinking has its roots firmly in the tradition that was initiated by Aquinas, and it should not surprise us that the dominant theme of Kierkegaard's philosophy is his struggle to articulate and perpetuate his Christian faith. The connection here to our discussion is obvious however indirect, namely, that in several ways, " 和 " is a fundamentally dialectical concept.

Finally, let us return to one of the theoretical concepts we have neglected thus far, namely Althusser's concepts of "contradiction and over-determination." Let me note that I am never interested in theory for the sake of theory, and thus, I am willing to take risks when trying to apply theories productively to situations that were not necessarily part of the thinking that inspired such theorizing in the first place. Nonetheless, while I will offer a somewhat original application of the theory here, I do not think it is very radical or controversial, although some would probably disagree with me on all accounts.

You may recall that Althusser examined by way of Lenin and Mao the various factors that led to Bolshevik success. Of course, looking at the October Revolution and all that followed entails analyzing historical facts including the very physical and undeniable aspects associated with armed struggle and the taking and losing of human life. I too will talk about revolution, or at least, the potential for revolution, but what I have in mind is the development of a potentially revolutionary discourse, one that might emerge as a revolutionary epistemological tradition, one that might bring together positively the good lessons from the East and West and therefore be in a position to make contributions to human progress as a whole.

Lenin argued that Russia was the "weakest link" in the Western imperial system, and I would like to argue that China might be the weakest link today in the Western epistemological tradition. I believe that there exists today in China and beyond the sort of contradictions and crises necessary to form what Althusser termed a "ruptural unity." In other words, the time is ripe for a revolutionary change in thinking, and thus, an epistemological revolution against the hegemonic Western epistemological tradition. This does not mean, I think, that some sort of traditionalist or nationalist turn inward or towards the past should be embraced. Rather, the focus needs to be on the future, but grounded historically. What I have in mind, in fact, is more of a progressive position than a conservative one; however, it would seem that one must consider the dialectical aspects of a progressive/conservative contradiction as yielding potentially positive developments.

As we have already noted, China has had a century to consider and in some cases adopt and adapt Western thinking to Chinese conditions and needs. This experience is one that we should study and learn from China. At the same time, while many in the West have studied many aspects of Chinese culture, language, philosophy, history, cuisine, and so on, it is clear that the West has not learned much as a whole from China. And here again, I think the West should learn the dialectic from China, and further, that those in China who have forgotten or neglected it should do the same.

Index

Printed in the United States
By Bookmasters